D1313922

# An Illustrated Guide to the

# Tarot

RE DI COPPE

RE DI DANARI

RE DI BASTONI

RE DI SPADE

REGINA DI COPPE

REGINA DI DANARI

REGINA DI BASTONI

REGINA DI SPADE

CAVAL. DI COPPE

CAVAL. DI DANARI

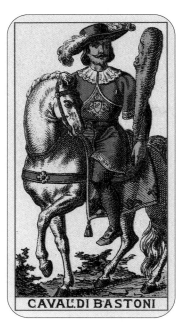

CAVAL. DI BASTONI

CAVAL. DI SPADE

# An Illustrated Guide to the

# Tarot

## Jonathan Dee

GRAMERCY

This 2001 edition is published by Gramercy Books™, an imprint of
Random House Value Publishing, Inc., 280 Park Avenue, New York,
NY 10017, by arrangement with D&S Books, Cottage Meadow, Bocombe,
Parkham, Bideford, Devon, England, EX39 5PH.

Gramercy Books™ and design are trademarks of Random House Value
Publishing, Inc.

Printed in Singapore.

Random House
New York • Toronto • London • Sydney • Auckland
http://www.randomhouse.com/

A catalog record for this title is available from the
Library of Congress

ISBN: 0-517-16398-5

987654321

# CONTENTS

# INTRODUCTION

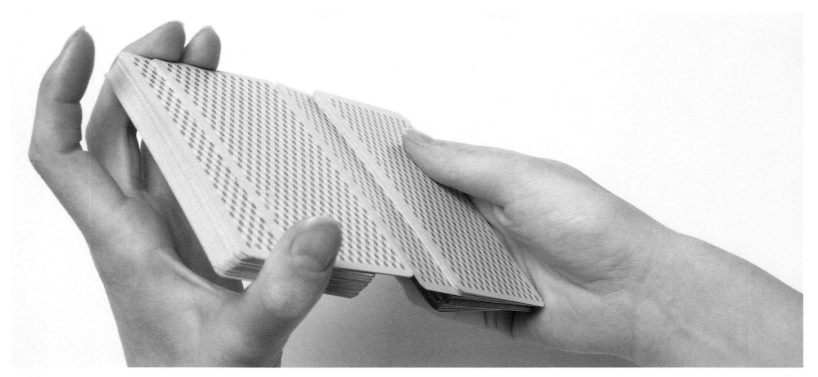

*It is very important to become familiar with your cards. Shuffle them every day and carry them about with you so that they can absorb your personal energies.*

With their complex imagery and occult symbols, Tarot cards have a colorful history as agents of fortune. There are many theories as to the origins of the Tarot, from ascribing them a great antiquity in ancient Egypt and Greece to a heritage in China and India. The first written evidence of their existence, however, is attributed to a fourteenth-century monk named Johannes of Brefeld who, evidently irritated by the great popularity of the Tarot, infamously referred to it as "the Devil's picture book." He was the first of a long line of churchmen publicly to denounce the cards, yet this condemnation did little to diminish their appeal. Throughout the last 700 years these enigmatic cards have lived on, and have been in continuous use for the purposes of gaming and divination.

The 78 cards of the classical Tarot deck consist of two packs of cards combined into one. These are called the Major Arcana (of 22 cards) and the Minor Arcana (of 56 cards). The word "Arcana" is taken from Latin and means "secret." (For the academically-minded, you could therefore term each individual card an "arcanum." This is certain to impress at dinner parties, but it is best to learn the traditional names for all your Tarot cards first.)

*Ancient Divining Tarot.*

*Esoteric Ancient Tarot.*

## Get to Know Your Cards

There are many customs about acquiring and keeping Tarot cards, but thankfully you can ignore most of them. Have you been told that it is unlucky to buy your own deck, but that it is also unlucky to be presented with a deck as a gift? Unless you hope your deck to materialize by magic, the most important issue is not superstition but personal appeal. A deck of cards that "resonates" for you, making you feel stimulated and inspired when you handle them, will act as a springboard for your intuition and psychic abilities. Choose a deck you like.

Consider all the images on your cards. Familiarize yourself by shuffling them every day, and carry them about with you. You might even want to sleep with them by your bed so that they can absorb some of your energy, and feel more uniquely yours. It's also best not to allow anyone else to play with your cards or handle them without your permission, and in particular no one but you should read with your deck without your blessing. They are your cards, so always remember that they are special.

Part of this specialness can be expressed in the way you keep the cards when they are not in use. Traditionally, cards are kept wrapped in black silk in a wooden box to preserve them from hostile vibrations. However, as Tarot cards hold a unique place in your consciousness, it is best to keep them safely in a place that is special to you. I keep my Tarot cards in a blue silk bag which was given to me by a Tibetan lama whom I met in the U.S.A. some years ago.

You may find that with repeated use the cards become so personal to you that they will only answer your questions and therefore eventually become useless when attempting a reading for another person. Fortunately there is no rule that states you cannot have more than one deck, so purchase another and repeat the familiarization process. To speed this up, you might consider laying out the new deck and placing the equivalent card from your old one on top of it. Then both new and old Tarot decks can be put away together safely.

*The Dee-Loren Tarot.*

# How to Use This Book

RE DI COPPE

REGINA DI COPPE

*The Tarot deck used to illustrate this book is the beautiful, but little known, Ancient Italian Tarot. However, the instructions and interpretations of the cards given within the book are suitable to any traditional Tarot pack of 78 cards.*

Chapter three gives a range of different layouts to try, followed by information on how to "time" your readings – to gain an understanding when events will take place.

Finally, don't worry if you initially find it difficult to interpret more than a few cards at a time. Any new skill needs a little patience and application. As with learning to play the piano, when reading Tarot cards practice does make perfect.

Chapter one outlines the upright and reversed meaning of all the Major Arcana cards. As you lay out your cards, some of the cards will fall upright, whereas others will fall upside down; simply read the interpretation that reflects the position of your card. Also included are tips on reading a Major Arcana card when it is placed near other key Major Arcana cards. This information gives you deeper insight into the meaning of a card. These "combinations" stem from the Italian Tarot tradition, and are included where appropriate.

Chapter two introduces the cards of the Minor Arcana. They are organized not by suit, but by type – for example, all of the fours, fives, and sixes are grouped together. This is to make the book even more accessible, and also to give you an insight into the numerological significance of the Minor Arcana cards, which can be difficult to interpret.

FANTE DI COPPE

CAVAL: DI COPPE

# Introduction to the Major Arcana

The 22-card Major Arcana, also known as the Tarot trumps, stands alone from the Minor Arcana. It does not belong to any of the four suits of the Minor cards, and there is some evidence that it may have developed separately, then been added to the Minor cards in the fifteenth century. The Major cards each have a title (alternative versions are given where appropriate) and they are numbered from I to XXI. Roman numerals are usually given on these cards in preference to everyday Arabic numbers to indicate the antiquity of their symbols. There is also an unnumbered card, called The Fool, which in some decks is numbered zero. The Fool is the only Major Arcana card to be translated into modern playing cards, now known as the Joker.

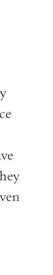

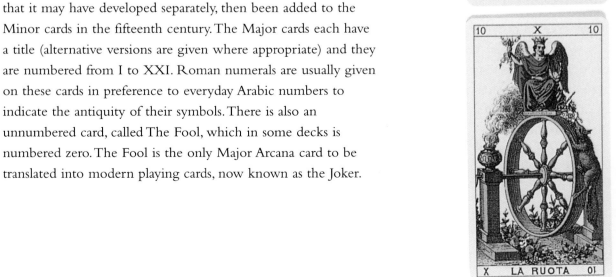

# The Meaning of the Symbols

When Major Arcana cards appear in your reading, they indicate a significant event or decision – practically, emotionally, and possibly spiritually. Unlike the everyday nature of the Minor cards, these Major cards point to influential change. Like the origins of the Tarot as a whole, there is much debate over the Major Arcana symbols. Some commentators believe them to be derived from ancient Egyptian hieroglyphics, while others ascribe to them an origin in India or China. Attention has been drawn to the fact that the 22 cards seem to have a connection with the 22 letters of the Hebrew alphabet, each of which has a mystical association in the Jewish occult system known as the cabbala.

The Major cards have also been allied to the signs and planets of astrology. Over the centuries, there have been numerous theories on how the cards and the celestial influences tie up. However, in the late nineteenth century, an occult brotherhood called the Hermetic Order of the Golden Dawn drew up a list of associations which is nowadays the most generally accepted, regardless of its inconstancies and peculiarities. For instance, the Fool is allocated the Air element, the Hanged Man, Water, and Judgement, Fire, but where is the fourth element, Earth? Equally strange is the association of the Moon with the High Priestess when there is a Moon card in the pack. There follows the Golden Dawn list of astrological and cabbalistic attributions.

# Astrological Attributions
*(Element, Planet, Zodiac Sign)*

|     |                    |                     | Hebrew Letter |
| --- | ------------------ | ------------------- | ------------- |
| 0   | The Fool           | Air, Uranus         | aleph         |
| I   | The Magician       | Mercury             | beth          |
| II  | The High Priestess | The Moon            | gimel         |
| III | The Empress        | Venus               | daleth        |
| IV  | The Emperor        | Aries the Ram       | he            |
| V   | The Hierophant     | Taurus the Bull     | vau           |
| VI  | The Lovers         | Gemini the Twins    | zain          |
| VII | The Chariot        | Cancer the Crab     | heth          |
| VIII | ★Justice          | Libra               | lamed         |
| IX  | The Hermit         | Virgo               | yod           |
| X   | The Wheel          | Jupiter             | kaph          |
| XI  | ★Strength          | Leo                 | tet           |
| XII | The Hanged Man     | Water, Neptune      | mem           |
| XIII | Death             | Scorpio             | nun           |
| XIV | Temperance         | Sagittarius         | samekh        |
| XV  | The Devil          | Capricorn           | ayin          |
| XVI | The Tower          | The planet Mars     | pe            |
| XVII | The Star          | The sign of Aquarius | tzaddi       |
| XVIII | The Moon         | The sign of Pisces  | qoph          |
| XIX | The Sun            | The Sun             | resh          |
| XX  | Judgement          | Fire, Pluto         | shin          |
| XXI | The World          | Saturn              | tau           |

★It is because of the attribution of Card VIII, Justice, to Libra and Card XI, Strength, to Leo that these cards sometimes swap places in modern Tarot decks.

# O The Fool
## *(The Joker)*

O     IL MATTO     O

## Upright Meaning

Because it is unnumbered, the Fool can be read as the first or the last card of the Major Arcana. As the first card, it acts as a preliminary to the cycle of cards that starts with the Magician, and therefore has strong associations with childhood and new beginnings. The Fool's fresh-faced optimism and sense of wonder are coupled with a fearlessness and *naïveté*. It is said that "Fools rush in where angels fear to tread," and this is precisely the case with this card. However, it is the innocence of his carelessness that protects him. The Fool's head is in the clouds, the Sun is in his eyes, and his mind is full of dreams, so he doesn't notice the pitfalls and dangers around him – and, in turn, they don't notice him.

When the Fool appears, there is a new road to travel. You might not know where it will lead you, but the prospect of the journey is exciting and the potential for fun is endless. Of course, you will learn along the way and will turn innocence into experience, yet the adventure will be worth every trial and mishap. Go forward with confidence, because now is your time to discover the wonderful eccentricities of the universe. If this card turns up in a position in a reading that represents another person, then prepare to encounter one of the oddest, most eccentric, and totally original individuals that you have ever met.

If this card appears as the first one in a reading, then you must exercise caution. Medieval Italian tradition suggests that if the Fool is the first one out of the pack, then the question that you are asking is probably the wrong one. It may be that you are asking it for wrong reasons or that you are mistaken in your initial assumptions.

## Reversed Meaning

The reversed meaning of the card is an exaggeration of the Fool's upright qualities, although here there is a warning against impulsive decisions and actions that border on folly. You may be acting in an immature or irrational manner, so apply some common sense.

When upright, the Fool suggests that you may as well leap before you look, but when reversed, the situation is more serious – take a brutally realistic overview at what lies before you. Otherwise, you could become the fool in every sense.

Reversed: some Tarot readers suggest that there may be a sexual problem of some kind when the card is found in the reversed position. A question of gender identity, or perhaps a confusion of roles, may be indicated. In a more general sense, if the Fool reversed is the first card out of the pack, then it is certain that you are embarking on a journey that is unwise to say the least, so think again.

# I The Magician
## *(The Juggler, the Magus)*

## Upright Meaning

First and foremost, this card is numbered I, so it shows initiative, new circumstances, new beginnings, and great hopes for the future. The Magician indicates a sense of purpose and the use of willpower.

(In some Tarot spreads [see pages 100-19] it is used to represent the questioner, if male – Card II, the High Priestess, is often used for women.) If the reading is for a woman and the Magician appears, the card represents the man in her life.

More generally, the Magician is a dynamic, forward-looking individual, who symbolizes many new opportunities. However, there is an element of uncertainty about the card. After all, new starts are often beset with teething troubles. Yet, with a little wisdom and foresight, the indications are that you will succeed in whatever you do.

The Magician has a mercurial nature, so being able to think on your feet, with perhaps the odd bluff or two, will get you through any initial difficulties. If you are considering a new enterprise, the appearance of the Magician shows that your plans have considerable potential, and it challenges you to get them off the ground.

If you are faced with opposition, then the appearance of the Magician is an excellent omen. The wily and mercurial nature of the card ensures that you will be at least three steps ahead of your rivals and will be able to out-talk, out-think, and outmatch them at every turn. Your moves will tend to be shrewd and fast. They may even have a trace of ironic humor about them, too.

## Reversed Meaning

The swift-thinking, fast-talking nature of the Magician takes a more sinister turn when the card is in the reversed position. Now the card may indicate a con artist, extremely plausible lies. and far-reaching deception. If a new enterprise is presented to you by others, be very suspicious. Question the motives of those around you.

## Combinations

The concepts of the new and the novel touch any card that is combined with the Magician. The new positive links are with any of the aces of the Minor Arcana, and also with the Sun, the Chariot. and the Wheel of Fortune. Even when combined with fairly negative cards, such as the Tower, the Magician suggests the overcoming of great difficulties. Also, take note of any of the court cards that appear with the Magician, because they could represent people who will help or hinder a new enterprise

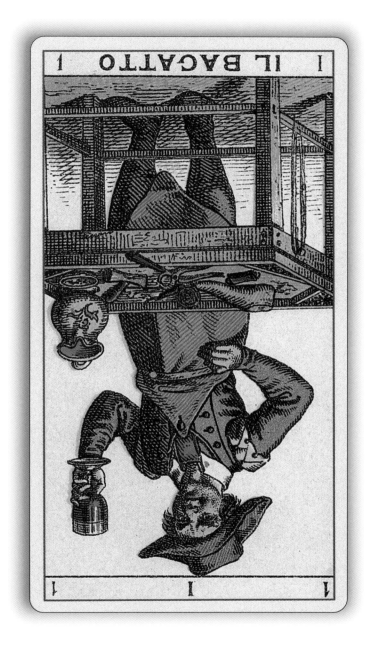

## II  The High Priestess
*(The Papess, the Female Pope, Juno )*

### Upright Meaning

The enigmatic figure of the High Priestess is the guardian of secrets, one of which is about to be revealed when this strange card turns up in a reading. When trying to interpret the card, the first thing to understand is that you do not yet have all of the facts at your disposal, even if you think that you do, and a little help from a wise guide will be a welcome development. Obviously, the card shows a strong feminine influence (In some Tarot spreads [see pages 100-19], it is used to represent the questioner, if female – Card I, the Magician, is often used for men.) Qualities that are traditionally considered feminine are symbolized by the High Priestess: intuition, memory, instinct, and psychic ability.

The scholarly aspect of the card is a signal to go ahead with studies that deepen the understanding of the universe and human nature. If you need to make a major decision, the arrival of the High Priestess shows that your gut feelings will be your best guide. There is also a suggestion that these instincts mask spiritual guidance from a higher power. In a man's reading, the High Priestess often represents a lady who is important to him. It can also symbolize inspiration, especially that which comes from his muse, or the woman in his life.

The veil that hangs behind the seated figure is about to lift a little, just enough to reveal a secret that you may suspect exists, but has remained hidden from you. How you deal with this new knowledge is up to you, but the enigmatic smile of the High Priestess suggests that you will have all the intuitive wisdom you will need to put it to the best possible use.

## Reversed Meaning

When reversed, stupid, careless remarks can wound, and secrets that should be kept are needlessly revealed. Common-sense attitudes fall by the wayside as passions boil over, possibly because you have spent so much time looking after other people's welfare rather than your own. Sexual tension and frustrations can make life a nightmare when the usually cool, collected High Priestess is found in the reversed position.

## Combinations

Combined with the Magician, a deep love seems to be developing. With the Emperor, it is a sign that the time for action has come, and, with the Fool, the card opens the doorway to total freedom, when literally anything is possible. However, if the High Priestess is found with the Empress and either of them is reversed, you will experience great confusion through emotional indecision.

# III   The Empress

## Upright Meaning

The appearance of the beautiful Empress signals a time of prosperity, joy, and love. Material comfort and great happiness is in store. The card is associated with springtime, and therefore with the fruitfulness of the earth and human fertility; pregnancy is often indicated by the appearance of this card. The maternal nature of the bountiful Empress is also expressed as a protective influence, indicating emotional support and the resultant feeling of security.

The Empress is a card of reassurance and love. It shows that things will work out alright for you in the end, and that you can be sure that whatever else happens, you are indeed held in deep affection. In some cases, the Empress can indicate moving to a new home, especially if you enjoy decorating, gardening, growing your own produce, or love surrounding yourself with beautiful possessions. There is a certain proprietary side to the card, too; in this sense, the mantra of the Empress could be "This is mine."

This card also has strong associations with the arts. If you have ambitions to create a masterpiece, compose a great symphony, or publish an earth-shattering novel, then the Empress smiles on your endeavors. Of course, your aspirations don't have to be that lofty, but, even so, the Empress promises success and tremendous enjoyment of the very act of creation.

## Reversed Meaning

The maternal Empress turns out to be too protective for comfort when the card is reversed. Emotional blackmail and domestic tyranny are the problems to watch out for when the card is in this position. There may be money problems and a need to be more careful with finances. There could be problems with children.

## Combinations

Close to the World, the Empress promises complete emotional fulfillment, but with the Tower or the Moon, it signals frustrations, inner conflict, and the possible breakup of a relationship. With the Hanged Man, it advises a lowering of emotional defenses and more spontaneity in your love life. The happiest card combinations for the Empress are reserved for the Sun, the aces of Wands, Cups, and Pentacles, and any of the pages of the Minor Arcana. A happy pregnancy and the arrival of a longed-for child are often shown when any of these occur in proximity to the fertile Empress.

# IV    The Emperor

## Upright Meaning

The Emperor means that you can be sure that high achievement and honors are on the way to you. This very masculine, regal figure represents the fulfillment of ambition. This is the card of people in authority, employers, managers, and sometimes politicians. Often, in a woman's reading, the Emperor may stand for a strong man in her life, such as a husband, father, or other paternal figure in whom she places her trust. Indeed, the Emperor may indicate the influence of a powerfully placed, influential man who has taken an interest in the questioner.

If the question asked is about love, then the appearance of the Emperor in a woman's reading suggests that a man in her life will stand by her and give her the support she needs. A similar interpretation applies when any partnership issue is inquired about: strong, steady support and the ability to cope with anything are the gifts of this card. If the Emperor appears in a position that refers to you, then you will have the power to influence people and events. You will emerge as a person of authority and trust. This may indicate moving up the ladder of society and achieving considerable status in life.

If you have felt somewhat despondent or lacking in confidence, then the appearance of the Emperor card shows that this period will soon end. It also indicates that you will possess some ability or talent that will lift you from your gloom and set you on the road to achieving your ambitions. If you have been the victim of ill will, be assured that you will triumph, but you must remember to be magnanimous in your hour of victory.

## Reversed Meaning

The Emperor shows a tyrannical side when the card is reversed. The authority he wields when upright has now become repressive and possibly abusive. The reversed card may show that ambitions will remain unfulfilled and that the status that is craved for will remain beyond your reach for a while. If you wish to know whether someone whom you have in mind is trustworthy, then the appearance of the reversed Emperor is an indication that he or she is not. If the reversed card is in part of the spread that refers to you personally, then perhaps you are not as strong and forceful as you would like others to think.

## Combinations

Paired with the Magician, the Emperor promises total success in all new ventures. With Death, there will be a need to make a completely new start. A combination with the Star shows clear vision and great insight, but with the Devil it warns of excessive pride followed by misfortune. Combined with any of the four kings of the Minor Arcana, the Emperor shows the character of the influential man that the card represents.

# V   The Hierophant
*(The High Priest, Jupiter, the Priest, the Pope)*

## Upright Meaning

The appearance of this subtle card in a reading suggests advice, wise counsel, and spiritual consolation. The Hierophant expresses the higher ideals of established religious systems. The card may also represent a teacher who may be a practical instructor, as well as a spiritual or philosophical guide. The Hierophant may be a real person who fulfills this guiding role, but this is unusual. More commonly, the card refers to a set of events that serve to give moral guidance. In short, the Hierophant represents the essence of convention, the tried and true, traditional values, and propriety. So if the card turns up as the answer to a question involving a novel concept, as opposed to an accepted code of behavior, then conventional thinking will win through every time.

If you are looking for someone in whom you can safely place your trust, then older, more staid individuals are those that the card recommends. The issues of right and wrong are usually very important when the Hierophant appears. Your judgement may be flawed, and you could find it difficult to make the right decision. In this case, conventional wisdom should prevail and the well-worn path of righteousness should be followed.

The card is also considered one of the indicators of marriage. If a less formal relationship is envisaged, you can be sure that there will be considerable outside pressure to make the union official in the traditional sense. The appearance of the card may also point to legal responsibilities, contractual agreements, and official documents.

## Reversed Meaning

Other people's opinions could be playing too much of a role in your decision-making when the Hierophant is reversed. Perhaps tradition is holding you back or preventing you from being the person whom you truly are. The stifling effects of an outworn set of values may be crippling new thinking. The card may also represent a crisis of faith, possibly leading to disorderly or uncharacteristic excesses.

On a more positive note, the reversed Hierophant may mean making your own decisions in defiance of established traditions, a rejection of bad advice, or striking out on your own.

## Combinations

Combined with the Tower, the Hierophant shows a tragedy precipitating a crisis of faith. Together with Death, it indicates a profound transformation in thinking and beliefs. With the Star, there is a need to start putting your ideas into action.

# VI  The Lovers

## Upright Meaning

The Lovers card is quite complex, as can be imagined where affairs of the heart are concerned. A literal interpretation is that love is coming into your life soon: a new lover, a new relationship, and emotional commitment are foretold. Even if love affairs are the last thing on your mind, you are in for a surprise. The card also reveals that the time has come to make an important choice that will affect the rest of your life.

The conflict here is established duty versus your heart's true desire. Two paths lie before you: one is a risk, but the payoff is great happiness and emotional fulfillment. The other course merely promises to continue your life in the way that you have previously known. One way offers excitement, the other a calm, controlled life of the familiar that is bound to become boring sooner or later. When making your decision, don't let logic color your thinking. On a less profound note, the card may also show a good partnership or a close friendship that touches your emotions.

The most important point to consider when dealing with this card is that the heart, not the head, will dominate any issue. Even if your final decision seems to throw caution to the wind, you can be sure that it is the right one and will lead you to a greater happiness than you would otherwise have known.

## Reversed Meaning

An unhappy love affair, dissatisfaction, and an unfulfilling life are shown when the Lovers card is reversed. The lifestyle choice of the upright position still lies before you, but do you have the courage to make it? There may be a separation from a loved one when the card appears in this position, but this need not be permanent, although it will be very unwelcome at the time. A sense of duty is strong when the card is reversed, and this may stand in the way of emotional and physical happiness.

## Combinations

When combined with any aces, or with either the Magician (male) or the High Priestess (female), it signifies the beginning of an intense love affair. It's the start of something exciting and intense. Paired with the Moon, it shows the danger of being led astray. Lust is the keyword when it is found with the Devil – the possibility of a relationship that is passionately sexual, but offers little spiritual fulfillment. With the Sun or the World, perfect happiness will be yours.

# VII  The Chariot

## Upright Meaning

The martial appearance of the Chariot signals that there are battles to be fought, considerable odds to be overcome, and that resilience of character will be needed if you are to achieve a victorious conclusion to your struggle. However, it is probable that the card is not foretelling anything new – this struggle has been going on in your life for some time already, and the Chariot's appearance in a reading encourages you to continue your efforts. It also signals unexpected good news that will boost your motivation, increase your optimism, and provide a sense of all being worthwhile.

Self-reliance and decisive action are the key concepts of the card, so prepare for renewed action. The card shows that you are the master of your fortunes and can steer your life in the right direction. Also, the Chariot can often be taken literally as a vehicle. Perhaps you will purchase a new automobile or undertake a journey by railroad or airplane. If the card expresses this traveling aspect, then it is likely that your journey will be related to work and duty rather than pure pleasure.

The card may also provide a gentle warning about excessive pride. The image of a crowned warrior in a chariot is reminiscent of Roman generals who paraded triumphantly through their conquered cities. These mighty warlords were reminded to act with humility and to remember that they were only mortal. Perhaps this message is implied when the Chariot appears in a reading.

## Reversed Meaning

The martial Chariot takes on a more arrogant aspect when it is reversed. Your ego may be out of control and you could easily be inflating your own self-importance out of all proportion. You may be rather frustrated and feel under pressure, causing you to lose your temper and direct your wrath toward those who do not deserve it.

You may feel that your life is not going in the direction that you would wish. You are likely to experience delays and obstacles to your progress, and travel plans will may go awry, much to your annoyance. Some calming meditative techniques may help when the Chariot is in the negative position.

## Combinations

When found with the Hermit, the Chariot indicates making a deep, heartfelt commitment. With the Moon, it may show errors of judgement. With Justice, the time has come to embark on a major enterprise.

# VIII Justice
## *(Adjustment)*

## Upright Meaning

The meaning of this card is self-evident: the card of Justice means justice, logic, fairness, and equilibrium in all dealings with others. It is therefore fortuitous for partnership issues. Justice also points the way to the giving or receiving of good advice, and indicates that decisions made by powerful people will work in your favor. The card promotes a sense of balance and harmony of a cool, intellectual kind. It may indicate the signing of contracts that will be beneficial to you, success in all legal affairs, and advantageous business proposals.

One aspect of the card that is often ignored is that it denotes the righting of a wrong that has been done to you in the past, or a crusading zeal on your part to see justice done on behalf of another. When the Justice card turns up, issues of honesty, loyalty, and idealism are paramount.

This card may also operate on a more spiritual level as the workings of positive karma. In other words, you may be justly rewarded for good deeds done in the past. In this circumstance, you can expect a run of good luck, though in all probability you will have no idea why you are being so favored. However, you can be sure that in some mysterious way the cosmic balance is being righted.

## Reversed Meaning

Literally the opposite of the upright meaning, the reversed Justice is usually interpreted as injustice. A decision will go against you, even if you are morally in the right. Legal matters are not so well aspected when this card appears in the negative position. False accusations may be made, and you could suffer from some form of prejudice or oppression. It is also wise to choose your advisors with more care, because much of the information that they pass on to you will be misguided or prompted by self-interest.

## Combinations

When placed near the Hermit, some deep thought in solitude will yield the logical answers that you need. Spiritual development is indicated by a link with the Hanged Man. Dark forces will be defeated when paired with the Devil, the Tower, and the Moon (the latter showing a struggle with conscience, too). A combination with the Fool indicates the sensible use of total freedom.

# IX   The Hermit
*(The Monk, the Veiled Lamp, the Traitor)*

## Upright Meaning

The meaning of the Hermit card is a subtle one. Obviously, its interpretation is linked with solitude and deep thought, yet this is not necessarily achieved through a physical withdrawal from society. It may be that some solace will be found within oneself, even when one is in company. You may feel the need to live quietly for a while and to let the hustle and bustle of the world pass you by to give yourself the opportunity to put your thoughts in order.

Another association of the card is with old age and the wisdom that is gained through experience. It may indicate the passage of time, showing that whatever issue is on your mind, it will take a while to be resolved. The card may stand for caution, showing a need for patience. The advice of the card is to develop a prudent attitude, to take your time, and not to rush headlong at anything. You are likely to realize that there is always something new to learn, and this lesson may be found in the words of someone with age and wisdom on their side. In health matters, the card indicates a time of convalescence.

Whenever this card turns up, there will be a slowing-down of events. If the Hermit is surrounded by positive cards, then this delay will eventually work out to your benefit and may even show that you are being prevented from making a far-reaching error. The Hermit may also give you the chance to think things over in a cool and deliberate frame of mind.

## Reversed Meaning

The wisdom and caution of the upright card vanish when the Hermit is reversed. Rash folly and impatience are raging,, and issues surrounding age also come into play. There may be a hint of the negative aspects of old age, such as isolation and loneliness, or alternatively, the arrogance of youth disregarding the advice of those older and wiser. The appearance of the reversed Hermit may show the emergence of a cantankerous obstinacy in someone of any age, as well as forgetfulness and a petulant refusal of genuine help. The loneliness associated with the card may be the result of betrayal when the card is reversed.

## Combinations

When the Hermit is combined with Strength, pent-up energies within you can accomplish anything. When paired with the Tower, it is a warning that you could make a serious error of judgement. With the Moon or the Sun, inner wisdom, harmony, and the process of attaining self-knowledge are at hand.

# X    The Wheel of Fortune

## Upright Meaning

The Wheel of Fortune is an indicator of a stroke of luck that will leave you astonished. Your life is definitely about to take a turn for the better. When this arrives in a reading, fate takes a hand in your affairs and improves your fortunes, usually quite suddenly and unexpectedly. The workings of the Wheel of Fortune could be a mystery to you, yet you will undoubtedly benefit from them. It is an indicator that your current problems are nearing their end, usually with little personal input.

When this card is seen, small nuggets of luck, such as finding lost coins or an uncashed check, act as pointers to the greater good luck to come. Take special note of the area of a spread in which this card occurs to find out where your luck is coming from. Any timing cards surrounding this harbinger of good news are of special interest, too, because they will tell you when it is due to arrive. One note of caution: remember that what goes up must come down, and vice versa. It is the nature of a wheel to turn, so enjoy your luck while it lasts and bear in mind that the card merely represents a temporary phase in life.

You will be riding high for a while, but remember that it is fate, not personal initiative, that has placed you in such an advantageous position. If you are prudent, you will use this period of exceptional good luck to put something away for a rainy day and prepare for times when the smiling face of good fortune does not appear so readily.

## Reversed Meaning

Temporary bad luck is likely when the Wheel of Fortune is reversed. There may be a few unpleasant surprises, but it is in the nature of a wheel to turn, and you will find that eventually things will change for the better. Perhaps the rotation of the fateful Wheel of Fortune will be more obvious when the card is reversed, with constant ups and downs leaving you somewhat confused by the fast changes that are happening around you.

## Combinations

When the Wheel of Fortune is paired with the Chariot, urgent decisions are needed to make your luck certain. The opposite is the case when coupled with the Hermit, as cautious optimism is your best course. The Magician emphasizes the unexpected nature of the luck encountered, while Justice promises extraordinary events and a kind of renewal in your life.

# XI Strength
*(Fortitude, Force, Lust)*

## Upright Meaning

The most obvious meaning of this card is physical strength, yet this is not necessarily an indication of feats of endurance, but can be interpreted as the ability to withstand an enormous amount of pressure and to triumph over it. If you have been ill, then the appearance of this card is an indicator of rapid recovery. If you've been thinking of giving up a bad habit, such as smoking, then this card shows that you have the willpower necessary to do it.

If health is not an issue for you, then Strength may indicate a fight for what is right. This is a battle that you are well equipped to win. Your courage and determination are up to the challenge, and nothing should, or could, deter you from this course. Willpower, mental strength, and self-belief are fundamental issues here. However, when Strength turns up, you can be sure that you will triumph over spiteful, jealous people. You will defeat ignorance and oppression, so remember to reward yourself when the battle is over.

Forget your insecurities and self-doubt when the card of Strength appears in the upright position. You have challenges to face, obstacles to overcome, and enemies to defeat. Don't begin the battle by fighting yourself first. You know the right thing to do. Don't shy away from it. Now you must prove yourself, and improve your own self-esteem at the same time.

## Reversed Meaning

The determination shown by the upright version may be misplaced, and you may be pursuing the wrong goal. Alternatively, the card may show cowardice, a loss of nerve, and a readiness to give in when victory is in sight. It is equally likely that you may not be able to deal with your problems alone, and will need to rely on someone else to support you while you take the lead.

When Strength is reversed, the first battle you must fight is with your own insecurity or fear.

## Combinations

With the Hanged Man, Strength indicates an extraordinary ability to master any situation. Powerful alliances are signaled by a pairing with the Emperor, while difficult battles are shown when it is found with Death, the Devil, or any of the higher Sword cards. With the Fool, the combination warns of excessive rashness and foolishness being mistaken for courage.

# XII The Hanged Man

## Upright Meaning

This is one of the most enigmatic cards in the Tarot deck. The card depicts a man hanging upside down, suspended by one foot, usually looking rapturous. Traditionally, the card is said to represent the principle of self-sacrifice, of spiritual, rather than material, values. However, it may also represent a temporary reversal of fortune that turns the world on its head.

The confusion associated with the card is understandable if one considers the possibility that you have been looking at things in the wrong way. Once this is realized, then a change of perspective is advisable. It may be that you are unable to react to the changes in fortune around you, and will feel buffeted by the winds of fate for a while. If this is the case, accept it with good grace, because to attempt to do anything else would be a waste of effort. However, you can be sure that all will work out to your ultimate benefit. You will really need to muster patience during this passive phase. Very occasionally, the Hanged Man signifies illness. More usually it shows the need to let go, so that something greater can be gained.

This theme of sacrifice has a spiritual overtone. In many ancient religions, illumination was achieved through some sort of ordeal. Perhaps the Hanged Man represents a trial of passage as you move from one phase of life to another, more fulfilling one, increasing your awareness and developing your spirituality as you do so.

## Reversed Meaning

The reversed Hanged Man actually looks as if he is standing on one leg, which we might note now appears to be tethered to the spot. This can symbolize a desire to move forward, but an inability to let go of the past. You may also be manipulated by others, who are using emotional blackmail to get their own way.

Conversely, you may be trying this ploy and playing the part of the martyr for unworthy reasons of your own. Otherwise, ask yourself if you are being masochistic, punishing yourself needlessly for some imagined crime.

## Combinations

Self-control is the key to all of the Hanged Man's links to other cards. With the Empress, it is the emotions that need a firm hand; with Justice, a sense of objectivity is necessary. It is with the Moon that the card speaks most eloquently of spiritual values and tells you how difficult your karmic path is likely to be.

# XIII Death
*(Mortality, Transformation, Change, the Close)*

## Upright Meaning

This card is undoubtedly the one that causes the most consternation when it turns up in a reading, yet its interpretation isn't usually as sinister as implied by the grim, scythe-wielding, skeletal figure depicted in some decks. When the Death card turns up, it does herald a death, but in the broader sense of a way of life, outdated attitudes, a relationship, or a job. (It is true that very, very occasionally this card does indeed mean the death of somebody. However, this should not be too much of a surprise, as the person in question is likely to be very ill at the time.)

However the change is manifested, it is sweeping, usually shocking and unpleasant, but actually proves to be a blessing in disguise. The card serves to get rid of the old and restrictive so that the new may enter your life. The ordeal that the Death card represents will be a trial, yet once it is over you will be free and able to make a brand-new start.

Some traditions make much of the fact that the skeleton is the most resilient part of the physical structure. Likewise, the skeletal figure in the card suggests that though much may change, the underlying facts of importance will still remain. Only the dead wood is cut away by the ghoulish reaper. That which is worthwhile will indeed survive.

## Reversed Meaning

When reversed or surrounded by negative cards, the meaning is little different from the upright meaning. However, there is more of a sense of dread about the card. You may view any changes with horror and be prone to depression and anxiety. However, fate seems to be more flexible when the card is reversed, giving you a little more control than you would otherwise possess. It may be that circumstances force your hand into making drastic, but necessary, change. Unpleasant as this prospect may sound, the alternative of stagnation, boredom, and the ultimate loss of the spark of your personality is infinitely worse. Be brave when the Death card appears: it's time to show what you're made of!

## Combinations

When the Death card appears in conjunction with the Devil, it emphasizes the irreversible nature of the change that is to come. Combined with the ten of Swords, it indicates violence. When the card is next to the Moon, inner conflicts will occur, and, if it is close to the Magician, progressive, radical change will come, along with the potential benefits that this transformation will bring.

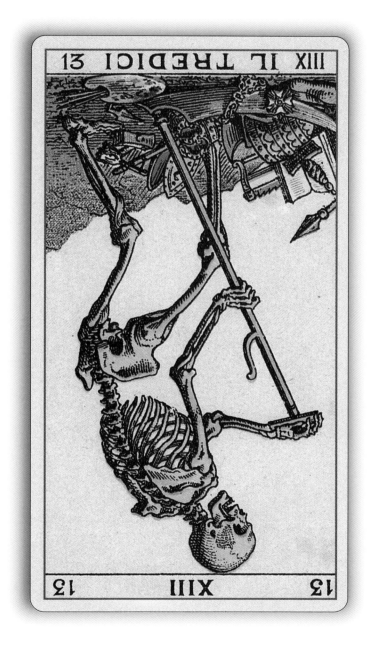

# XIV Temperance

## Upright Meaning

This gentle card is numbered 14, which places it between the dramatic influences of Death and the Devil. At first this may seem surprising, yet the card of Temperance often shows the careful control of difficult circumstances (symbolized by the other cards) and the deft handling of volatile factors. In essence, Temperance is a card of harmonious partnership, of putting things together, of mixing and matching to achieve the right result. Its virtues are those of self-control and adapting to changing circumstances.

If you have experienced a difficult time and have suffered because of the breakup of a relationship, bereavement, material hardships, or some other trouble or loss, then the appearance of Temperance is a welcome sign. Peace will soon be restored, your ills alleviated, and your troubles soon ended. A tranquil normality will again be a feature of your life, and you will learn to cope again.

Moderation is the key to happiness when this card turns up. If you have been overdoing anything, then soon good sense and calm will prevail. Spirituality may well provide comfort, and you can be sure that there is indeed someone up there who is looking out for you when this card appears in your reading.

## Reversed Meaning

Harmony is disrupted when Temperance is in the negative position. You could find yourself in a situation that makes you so busy that you cannot see where you are going or gain a true sense of perspective. You may have a rival who competes with you on every level and undermines your confidence. Quarrels and strife are likely, although the peaceful nature of the card hints that these may be short-lived. In this case, certain places and people may not be good for you, and, in some instances, very unfortunate. It also warns of corrupt dealings, misplaced ideals, and the possibility of domestic strife.

## Combinations

When this gentle card is found with the Magician, it can signify deep understanding and great wisdom. It has a similar, though more intuitive, meaning when it teams up with the Priestess. When paired with the Fool, a state of inner peace and tranquility will follow. Proximity to the Devil may show illness, while combined with the Star, it demands that you be more assertive and express your opinions in a forthright manner.

# XV  The Devil
*(Temptation, Pan)*

## Upright Meaning

The Devil card is not necessarily a bad card, because it can mean permanence, so it is a good sign if it appears when a marriage or committed partnership is under consideration. At other times, however, it does tend to show circumstances that are initially attractive, but will become an inescapable prison over the course of time. The card is associated with the temptations of the flesh, of a lust that gives no peace. It can therefore point to a passionate love affair or being held in the thrall of love by the wrong sort of person. Addictions of all sorts, pleasurable at first, yet ultimately destructive, are also indicated by this card.

The Devil may also signify greed and materialistic attitudes that allow no spiritual values to alleviate their negative effect on the soul. It is important to remember that the Devil is a tyrant who allows no independence of thought or vision.

The appearance of the card warns that you are refusing to see the destructive consequences of your own actions. The card may also indicate an immovable obstacle in your path. Direct confrontation will never work when the card appears in this way, so cunning and stealth will be your best defense against difficulties.

When the Devil card is prominent in a reading, question your motives. Are you doing something that is ultimately destructive, spiteful, or wounding to yourself or to others? If you find that this is so, the appearance of the card may signal your final opportunity to change course before it is too late.

## Reversed Meaning

The tyranny of the Devil card begins to crumble when the card is reversed. The bonds that once held you so tightly are just beginning to slacken enough to remind you what freedom feels like. In this position, the card may indicate the overcoming of bad habits, destructive thought patterns, and addiction. However, there is still some danger around. Don't involve yourself with people who have been a bad influence and choose your new friends with care. The last thing you need is to leave one prison and then to walk into another.

## Combinations

The lustful and compelling nature of the Devil card adds a perilous and addictive angle to any card that it is paired with. However, with the more negative cards, such as the Tower, its destructive nature is most evident. When close to this card, it warns of grave danger, but if either card is reversed, then it is probable that disaster will be averted.

# XVI The Tower

*(The Falling Tower, the Tower of Destruction, the Lightning-struck Tower, the Fire From Heaven, the House of God, the Hospital)*

## Upright Meaning

The positive side of this card is quite hard to find, although the disruptions that it predicts do indeed have a hint of freedom. Firstly, though, your sense of security is going to be seriously undermined. It may be that a whole value system is at the point of collapse and that you will be forced to reassess your life, your beliefs, and many of those things that you have relied upon. It is likely that this forced reassessment will occur suddenly, as the result of some disaster or tragedy. You may dread the shattering of your comfortable illusions, but the new reality that will emerge out of this seeming chaos can no longer tolerate them.

The going will be hard when this card turns up in a reading, but you can be sure that you will come out of the other side of the experience a stronger and more capable person. The Tower card opens doorways that you would never open by your own choice. In some ways, it takes the options away from you in the short term, but looking farther along the road of life, it opens up so many possibilities that you can scarcely imagine their scope.

After the Tower has fallen you may be left feeling somewhat bewildered. Take your time to plan your next course of action. You will be totally free to make up your own mind and to start again in the sure knowledge that you will not make the same mistakes again.

## Reversed Meaning

The initial indications of the reversed Tower may be even more disruptive than its upright meaning. You may be falsely accused of something; there may even be a form of imprisonment or forced isolation included in this oppression. On the other hand, you may be rebelling against some form of tyranny, showing a side of your personality that will come as a shock to others. In this case, it will be you who provides the disruptive surprises, who "rocks the boat" and refuses to bow down any more. Whether this rebellion is a good thing or a bad one should be revealed by the surrounding cards.

## Combinations

As might be expected, the Tower's influence on other cards is not usually a good one. When it is found with the Moon, it indicates the absolute impossibility of attaining your goal and urges you to think again. With the Sun, it may show the breakup of a relationship, which will nevertheless turn out to be a good thing. If found with the Fool, then to escape the worst effects of the card, adaptability and a readiness to take an unexpected escape route may save you from harm.

# XVII   The Star

## Upright Meaning

This is an extremely optimistic card, bringing hope, the renewal of faith, and unexpected gifts. Its positive message is quite clear: although you may have suffered setbacks and disasters in the past, your security will be restored. When the Star appears, problems will be solved, life will be smoother, and you will feel more lively and optimistic about your prospects. New enterprises begun under the auspices of this card have a very good chance of success. The exuberant message of the Star promises a happy outcome and many new opportunities.

There is often an artistic or educational matter to be considered, and the Star promises success in these endeavors. Pleasurable travel is often indicated by the card, so you may embark on a memorable vacation or just enjoy a light-hearted, vacation feeling. Good health or improvement in health is often shown, so this is an excellent omen if someone close has been ill. Spirituality and a sense that your life has meaning is the underlying theme of the Star, and you may experience an insight into a more mystical dimension when this card appears prominently in your reading.

It might be rewarding to take a special note of the Star's position in your reading, because its hopeful message will apply to that area of your life. If found in an area that refers to relationships, then the doorway of love is opening to you; if in a career position, then it is likely that a new, and more fulfilling, job is on its way.

## Reversed Meaning

Although positive, the future can appear quite tense when the Star is reversed or surrounded by less fortunate cards. The optimism of the upright Star is blighted by a lack of belief on your part, or by an apparent lack of opportunities. You may feel that you have been let down so often in the past that you refuse to hope any more. At the very least, the reversed Star shows much self-doubt. However, although your once-bright hopes seem to have been dashed, you will still be surprised by your good luck – despite your cynical attitude.

## Combinations

When combined with the Moon, there will be inner tensions that can be expressed and dealt with. Psychic power and spiritual revelations are indicted when paired with the High Priestess. With the Fool, it shows an open mind and a readiness to expand mental and spiritual horizons.

# XVIII The Moon

## Upright Meaning

When the Moon card appears in a reading, you can be sure that highly-charged emotions are causing havoc in someone's life. In this way, the Moon signifies illusion, because all is not as it seems when viewed through the filter of unruly emotion. The ability to step back, regain perspective, and regard your anxieties with a cool attitude is vital now. However, this is likely to be extremely difficult. The path that you are on is a hard one, full of twists and turns of fate, yet it is right for you.

Continue along your course, even when you are despondent and beset by doubt, because all will turn out for the best in the end. The wan light of The Moon, albeit weak and deceptive, does show the way, even if you lose sight of your long-term goal now and again. On another level, the Moon card is favorable for those engaged in a clandestine love affair.

On a more positive note, the Moon's interpretation as a card of illusion can actually be turned to good effect. The imagination will be powerfully stimulated at this time, and you may find yourself inclined to express it in a creative manner. You might want to reveal your inner self through art, writing, or music. Even the most troublesome emotional turmoil may yet inspire a work of genius.

## Reversed Meaning

Deception and trickery are in the air. The reversed Moon warns that you are being misled, and, unfortunately, those plaguing worries have a factual basis. Tradition has it that the card signifies hidden enemies and traps, so you will need to be very careful indeed to avoid their snares. Lies and insincerity are likely to be a feature of your life just now, so harden your heart and don't allow your desires to lead you to believe nonsense – no matter how much you want to! Needless to say, the Moon in this position is not so good for clandestine love. It's likely that your secret will be exposed.

## Combinations

The combination of the Moon and the Sun tends to show initial difficulties in establishing a relationship due to differences in the lifestyles of the partners. Traditionally, when paired with the Empress, feminine medical problems can occur, especially regarding conception. Be extra careful when this card is with the Wheel of Fortune, because accidents and sudden mishaps are likely.

# XIX The Sun

## Upright Meaning

The Sun is one of the best cards in the Tarot. It foretells good health, happy times, love, romantic fulfillment, children, and joy. The mood of the card is buoyant, uplifting, and extremely happy. The Sun can also signify the season of summer, or time spent in hot, sunny places. There may be good news about your offspring, or perhaps the birth of a child. Reunions with old and dear friends are likely, too, as are plenty of laughs and agreeable companionship.

Your difficulties will be overcome and triumph will be yours, perhaps accompanied by a measure of fame or at least a recognition of your achievements. Although the Sun card does not promise wealth *per se*, it does seem to create the conditions of prosperity. The card is also said to brighten the cards around it, so even if your reading seems full of gloom, the appearance of this card dispels negativity and promises a happy ending.

In keeping with the uplifting message of the Sun card, health issues that have been troublesome will soon see a remarkable improvement. In fact, the interpretation of the Sun card is so excellent that the events that it foretells may seem to be far too good to be true. However, you are about to be very pleasantly surprised.

## Reversed Meaning

Even when reversed or in a negative position, the Sun is not a bad card. There may be a few delays along the road, but the essential message remains the same: good times are on the way. The only drawback is that your success may go to your head a little – you may think that you have achieved everything all on your own and a touch of arrogance creeps in. On the other hand, you are likely to be right, even if a little immodest.

## Combinations

The appearance of the Sun in combination with any other card brightens the outlook, even if that card is particularly negative. There is one possible exception to this, and that is a pairing with the Moon, but even the uncertainty indicated by this will be overcome eventually. With the High Priestess, the Sun assures you that you are in the right, while with the Chariot, it makes victory absolutely certain. It is most dramatic when associated with Death: any changes signified by the Death card will bring almost incredible benefits to your life.

# XX Judgement
*(Resurrection, the Angel, the Aeon, Karma, Awakening)*

## Upright Meaning

The fanfare of Judgement sounds, and its clarion call cannot be ignored. It signals an end and a new beginning. Firstly, this is a card of logical conclusion, an end to work or the completion of a long-term venture. However, this is not a time for regret, but for rejoicing. Your job has been well done and your conscience is clear. Soon the rewards of your efforts will follow. You will rightly feel that you have done your duty and will be looking forward to the next phase of your life.

It is important to bear in mind that although this is the end of an important phase, there are bigger and better things to come, so new opportunities will present themselves when this card appears. These fresh chances will have far-reaching implications because they could change your life yet again in dramatic ways. This new lease of life will bring opportunities to do all of those things that have been put on hold because you were too busy and your attention was directed elsewhere. Traditionally, the appearance of the Judgement card is said to speed up the pace of events, so that whatever is foretold in your reading will occur more quickly than would otherwise be indicated. Another aspect of the Judgement card is associated with the law, so if you've had any legal disputes, then the card shows that these will be ruled in your favor.

## Reversed Meaning

The swift conclusions foretold by the upright card will be frustratingly delayed when Judgement is reversed. You may be frightened of the far-reaching changes ahead, ignoring new opportunities, and refusing to abandon your routine – although the future promises to be better.

Judgement reversed may indicate a denial of inevitable and desirable change. It is also said that a fear of illness, or even death, may prevent someone from seeking treatment or information about their condition when the card is in this position. When timing with the cards (see pages 120-25), a reversed Judgement often slows the pace of events.

## Combinations

If the Judgement card should appear in a reading before the Magician, the changes that the angel heralds will be accompanied by a far-reaching change of outlook and attitude to life. If the card following Judgement is the Fool, then free-thinking and originality will pay off in a big way. However, if the Death card is the immediate successor to Judgement, there will be an inability to face facts or to cope with change.

# XXI The World
*(The Universe, the Crown of the Magi)*

## Upright Meaning

At its very best, the appearance of the World signals the arrival of your heart's desire – whatever that might be! The longed-for reward promised by so many of the other cards is now imminent. Total success, happiness, and a feeling of justifiable pride are the gifts of this card, which is considered to be the very best in the Tarot deck. The triumph that you have sought so determinedly will now be appreciated by those who have witnessed the struggles that you have endured. Good friends and acquaintances will accord you the respect that you deserve. The final change is here, and you can now bask in the knowledge that you have done your best and won through.

For many people, the appearance of the World will be a signal to go out into it, to travel, and to enjoy the fruits of your labors on a well-deserved vacation. You might want to own part of the World by finally purchasing your dream home. In affairs of the heart, a wonderfully fulfilling relationship of perfect love is on offer. For some, the card will mean fame, worldly power, and far-reaching influence. For others, it will bring wealth. In short, the card foretells a time when your dearest dreams and most cherished ambitions will come to pass. Look at the cards surrounding the World to establish the nature of the reward that you will receive.

## Reversed Meaning

Since this is such a good card, its reversed interpretation cannot be too negative, so it usually means that you still have a little way to go before the promised rewards will be delivered. Don't lose heart now, or decide to change your direction this late in the day. Possibly, a sense of permanence has become more important to you, and an old ambition no longer seems to have the appeal that it once did.

You may be feeling insecure and dread the thought of making the final push to victory. If this is the case, then you need to start appreciating the improvements in your life that the World symbolizes. It may also be that you are envious of others' successes, yet are unwilling to make the effort to become more successful yourself.

## Combinations

If the World card is followed by the reversed Magician, then the atmosphere will be hectic, even possibly hysterical. This combination shows the need for calm and a clear head. If the Hierophant follows the World, then great spiritual progress is indicated. The same message is given by a combination with the Hanged Man, but in this case the probability is of some mystical illumination. However, when followed by the Chariot, the rewards that youwill receive will be considerable, yet you will also take on some very taxing duties.

# Introduction to the Minor Arcana

RE DI COPPE

FANTE DI COPPE

CAVAL. DI COPPE

RE DI DANARI

REGINA DI DANARI

CAVAL. DI DANARI

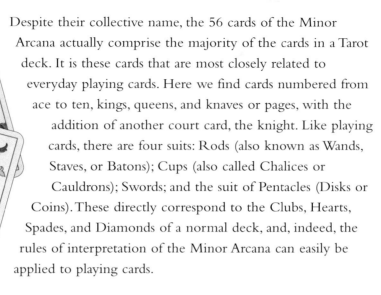

Despite their collective name, the 56 cards of the Minor Arcana actually comprise the majority of the cards in a Tarot deck. It is these cards that are most closely related to everyday playing cards. Here we find cards numbered from ace to ten, kings, queens, and knaves or pages, with the addition of another court card, the knight. Like playing cards, there are four suits: Rods (also known as Wands, Staves, or Batons); Cups (also called Chalices or Cauldrons); Swords; and the suit of Pentacles (Disks or Coins). These directly correspond to the Clubs, Hearts, Spades, and Diamonds of a normal deck, and, indeed, the rules of interpretation of the Minor Arcana can easily be applied to playing cards.

## The Origins of the Suits

By tradition, each of the four suits is identified with one of the four classical elements. The suit of Rods is usually ascribed to the Fire element (although some claim that it is airy in nature), Cups to Water, Swords to Air (but some say Fire), and Pentacles to Earth. Their symbols may also relate to the four classes of medieval society, Rods being used to describe the peasantry; Cups, the clergy; Swords, the nobility; and Pentacles, the merchants and storekeepers. The great Irish poet W. B. Yeats (1865–1939) also noted that the suits' symbols have a remarkable similarity to the four magical treasures of Celtic legend. These were the Spear of Lug (Rods), the Cauldron of the Dagda (Cups), the Sword of Nuada (Swords), and the Stone of Fal (Pentacles). With the coming of Christianity, these mutated into the four Grail Hallows, which were the Spear of Longinus (Rods), the Holy Grail itself (Cups), the magical Excalibur (Swords), and, finally, the Stone of Kings (Pentacles), which is often identified with the Stone of Scone upon which British monarchs are still crowned.

Minor Arcana cards generally refer to practical issues in a reading, and may be used separately or within the full Tarot deck.

# Interpreting the Court Cards

RE DI COPPE

REGINA DI COPPE

CAVAL. DI COPPE

FANTE DI COPPE

*Despite the similarity of the Minor Arcana to the modern deck of playing cards, there are four court cards in each suit. The familiar kings, queens, and knaves (or pages) are joined by mounted figures called knights.*

Although a Tarot beginner may find the imagery of the Major Arcana unfamiliar, and somewhat complex at first, the court cards can be deceptively difficult to interpret. This is because they generally represent real people who are known to you, or have yet to come into your life. Reading these cards does take practice. Firstly, because we are unique individuals, it is almost impossible to capture every facet of a personality within just one card. Secondly, these cards may also tell of specific events or changes linked to your emotional or spiritual development. And, to confuse matters further, in Tarot tradition there are a number of conflicting ideas about the types of people that these cards symbolize. Given these possibilities, it is not always easy to determine what a court card is actually saying in a reading.

Outlined on the following pages are some traditional descriptions that you can choose from or combine to help you to arrive at a final interpretation. If you are using playing cards, remember that there are 16 court cards in the Tarot deck – four kings, four queens, four knights, and four pages or knaves (or princesses, depending on which pack you happen to be using). Of course, ordinary playing cards have only 12 court cards, the knight and the page having been combined into the Jack.

The mounted figure of the knight was probably dropped as a separate card when playing cards became reversible. After all, it is difficult to fit both a horse and a rider into a pleasing playing-card design without simultaneously losing their feet. However, some playing-card readers actually add another, specially marked, Jack to their deck of cards to represent the lost knight.

# The Romany Method

*In the Romany method of card interpretation, the queens of the Minor Arcana represent mature women.*

Romany fortune-tellers use a simple interpretative method that can be applied to both Tarot cards and ordinary playing cards. According to the Romanies, kings are mature men who have some standing in the world; queens are likewise mature women; knights are young men making their way; and pages are children and young people of both sexes. If you are reading normal playing cards, you must combine the descriptions of the knight and the page.

In the Romany system, great emphasis is placed on the coloring of the person represented by a particular card. The court cards of the suits of Rods or Clubs are seen as brown-haired people with pale skin. Those of the suits of Cups or Hearts tend to be pale and blond. Swords or Spades court cards represent people who are dark haired with midtone skin, while those symbolized by Pentacles or Diamonds have dark complexions and tend to be shorter than those shown in the suit of Swords.

## Astological Method

Over the past few centuries there have been various attempts to link Tarot cards with the even more ancient art of astrology. The astrological system is based on the four suits of the Minor Arcana relating to the four classical elements of Fire, Water, Air, and Earth. Because each element is assigned three signs of the zodiac,

each court card can represent someone born under one of three signs. For example, court cards of Rods or Clubs represent people born under one of the Fire signs: Aries, Leo, or Sagittarius. Similarly, those born under one of the Water signs of Cancer, Scorpio, or Pisces would be represented by the court cards of Cups or Hearts. Air people born under the signs of Gemini, Libra, or Aquarius would be indicated by Swords or Spades. Finally, the Earth signs of Taurus, Virgo, or Capricorn would be depicted by the court cards of Pentacles or Diamonds.

If we now combine the Romany and astrological systems, we gain a fuller description of a person than one method alone could provide. For instance, the king of Pentacles might describe a swarthy, mature man with dark hair and eyes, born under an Earth sign. The page of Cups could be a blond, blue-eyed child, probably a Cancerian, Scorpio, or Piscean. However, even when these two methods are used together, they act as broad guidelines rather than giving specific detail, so you may need help from the "Roles" method described on the following page.

*Likewise, kings symbolize mature men who possess some authority.*

# The "Roles" or Career Method

Another method of reading the court cards looks at what the character in question does for a living, or the broader role that this person plays in your life. In this method, the king of Rods is a businessman, and the queen is equally independent about managing her own affairs. The knight of Rods is a young, ambitious professional, and the page a hard-working youngster.

The king of Cups is seen as an artistic or sensitive older man, and the queen a woman of the same nature. The knight of Cups is a lover, while the page is perceived as a quiet, rather withdrawn, young person.

In keeping with their ill-omened reputation, the Swords court cards show a harder edge. The king of Swords is often identified as a professional man, a doctor, judge, or lawyer. The queen may be a widow or divorcee, and possibly a tough or bitter character. The knight of Swords is a fickle ne'er-do-well who will turn your world upside down, while the page is suspected to be a sneak and a slanderer.

The court cards of the Pentacles suit generally refer to finance, land, and practicality, so the Pentacles king is a wealthy man, a landowner, banker, or other well-established business executive. The queen is an earth mother, while the knight of Pentacles is a capable and efficient worker. The poor page, though, is likely to be poverty-stricken, but with potential. He or she may be a student or an apprentice.

*In the "Roles" or Career method of card interpretation, the king of Swords could represent a doctor, lawyer, judge, or other skilled professional man.*

*The queen of Rods or Clubs is likely to be an independent women, quite often running her own business, as well as managing a family.*

RE DI SPADE

REGINA DI BASTONI

# Combining Methods

The eclectic systems of interpretation described here represent differing traditions in Tarot reading, but you can use all of these methods together to create a reasonably complete picture of the individual in question. For instance, if we return to the king of Pentacles, previously typified as a swarthy, dark, mature man born under one of the Earth signs, we can now add that he is likely to be comfortably off, probably with a good job and his own house. The same sort of composite picture can be created with any of the court cards. So now we'll move on to examining each of the court cards individually, to provide more complete character guidelines, as well as the potential events surrounding the person that the cards reveal.

It is important to remember that your intuition should be the final arbiter of the court cards. You may find that the person illustrated on the card itself is a true reflection of someone you have in mind, while in other cases it is not. Also, watch out for other court cards nearby, because their meanings may cast more light on a particularly elusive personality.

RE DI DANARI

REGINA DI SPADE

FANTE DI BASTONI

FANTE DI COPPE

*The court cards of the Tarot represent many different types of people. In some ways they can be thought of as rough caricatures of those whom you already know and those who will soon come into your life. By combining the various methods of interpretation, a fuller picture of each of these characters is possible.*

# The Aces

The aces represent beginnings. In numerology, the number one denotes the first impulse, so these are primarily action cards, each reflecting differing influences in our lives according to one of the four elements: Fire (the ace of Rods), Water (the ace of Cups), Air (the ace of Swords) and Earth (the ace of Pentangles). Potential, initiative, and dynamism are symbolized here, so when an ace appears in a reading, you can be sure that a new set of events is about to be set in motion.

## The Ace of Rods or Clubs

### Upright Meaning

The masculine ace of Rods is under the rulership of the creative Fire element. This card expresses initiative, drive, and the stirring of ambition, often relating directly to your working life and career – so expect new opportunities. An enterprise is on offer, such as a new job or stimulating leisure project. A broader interpretation of the ace of Rods as a masculine, creative force implies the birth of a child, as well as general good news and good fortune.

### Reversed Meaning

This card is so fortunate that it cannot really have a bad side. However, it can indicate a delay in events, or teach you that you are not quite as independent as you think. Consider your current plans as being perhaps too complex to be workable and simplify them and be more direct. The fiery nature of the card also warns against being tactless or obsessively singleminded.

## The Ace of Cups or Hearts

### Upright Meaning

The ace of Cups is the first card of a suit that is governed by the emotional element of Water. It is a feminine card, associated with bubbling springs, fountains, and tumbling waterfalls. This ace brings joy, love, and creative impulses that lead to great satisfaction. When this card appears, expect a new, exciting love affair, or at the very least a period of happiness. You will feel inspired and optimistic, and in return will receive emotional support from others. Good news about love, marriages, births, and other collective celebrations is the gift of this card.

### Reversed Meaning

Turbulent emotions and a lack of connection with other people occur when the ace of Cups is overturned. Self-confidence may be running low, creating feelings of loneliness and insecurity. Perhaps a relationship is not making you happy, or you now know that you may have pinned many a fond hope on someone who is not worthy of your love. When this card is reversed, you will need true affection to help you to regain your emotional equilibrium.

# The Ace of Swords or Spades

## Upright Meaning

When the ace of Swords appears in a reading, expect dramatic changes; as this card signifies an unstoppable, penetrating force. When wielding the sword, you can defeat any challenger, winning by the sheer power of your will. However, because the sword cuts both ways, you may need to make sacrifices in order to get what you desire. This Air card has a fearsome reputation, partly due to its link with death, but this only applies to the ending of a way of life rather than the demise of any person.

## Reversed meaning

The blade of the sword now points toward you, and is bound to wound in some way. At least expect misunderstandings, arguments, and delays to your plans. Even more worrying is the likelihood that your expectations and hopes will be dashed, causing you stress and anxiety about the future. You may react to this misfortune by being dictatorial and sarcastic. Try to regain your perspective by considering your options with calm and reason.

# The Ace of Pentacles or Diamonds

## Upright Meaning

The ace of Pentacles is governed by the fruitful element of Earth. It signifies gain and the opportunity to increase your finances. Although this ace may indicate a chance money win, it is more likely to signify long-term change. Promotion may bring you a more lucrative job and the material comforts of a higher income. The ace of Pentacles heralds contentment, security, and the end of financial worry, so enjoy this prosperous period.

## Reversed Meaning

"The best-laid plans of mice and men oft gang aglay," as Rabbie Burns once put it. New-found monetary fortune may not last. Beware of making bad investments, of gambling away your hard-earned cash, and of corrupt business dealings. Alternatively, a money-making scheme may be profitable, but is making you miserable. This card also points to greed based on emotional insecurity.

# Combinations

Traditionally, it is said that if only one ace appears in a spread, then a lack of focus is indicated. This is especially so if the ace is placed near negative cards, or is reversed. Conversely, if no ace appears, ask yourself if you are really clear about the nature of the question that you are asking the cards. If more than one ace appears in your reading, this also has a special significance: the closer they appear together, the more important this extra meaning will be. For instance, two aces signify partnership. A love affair or new home may be the outcome. The appearance of three aces represents good news in general, and all four aces in a reading emphasize new beginnings, dynamism, and potential.

# The Twos

In numerology, two is the number of harmony and balance. In Chinese mysticism, it is related to the concept of yin and yang, the balancing of positive and negative energies symbolized by the light and dark halves of a circle. In the Western world, two is traditionally regarded as a feminine number that either unites opposing forces or separates them irrevocably. Hence the twos of the Tarot deck present the reader with a choice between two alternatives, or they indicate the bringing together of people and events, often in unlikely circumstances. .

## The Two of Rods or Clubs

### Upright Meaning

A meeting of minds that results in a harmonious partnership is often shown by the appearance of the two of Rods. A working relationship will lead to success and prosperity. This card expresses the adage of great oaks and little acorns – humble beginnings that lead to unforeseen achievements. Promising developments in connection with property matters are also indicated. In fact, this card shows great potential in all areas of life, particularly work and friendship.

### Reversed Meaning

A partnership may be causing you more problems than it is worth. Reversed, this card often shows friction in a relationship that may, or may not, be resolved. Delays in financial transactions and frustration due to other people's incompetence are also highlighted. Questions of trust and pride may arise due to a partner's stubborn refusal to listen to reason. There could be an inability to adapt to rapidly changing circumstances.

# The Two of Cups or Hearts

## Upright Meaning

In keeping with the nature of this emotional suit, the two of Cups expresses the commitment of love as two people come together in mutual bonds of harmony and affection. This may be a case of opposites being very attractive to one another. However, when this link is not an affair of the heart, it can show a deep and abiding friendship, cooperation between individuals, and emotional contentment. A renewed understanding may develop and an old quarrel be finally resolved. The principal meaning, however, is love, so when this card appears in a reading, you can be sure that Cupid is playing fast and free with his arrows of romance.

## Reversed Meaning

Separation and a loss of sympathetic understanding are symbolized when the two of Cups is reversed. However, this separation may not be permanent, and could merely foretell a time when you and your loved one will be apart for purely practical, rather than emotional, reasons. When surrounded by negative cards, the two of Cups reversed can spell divorce. Either way, affairs of the heart are turned upside down, so you can expect a turbulent period in your love life.

# The Two of Swords

## Upright Meaning

Sword cards generally mean trouble and anxiety. However, as cards of this suit go, the two of Swords is not too negative. It may indicate a time of adversity, but it also promises friendship and support to help you to get through your difficulties. A verbal duel may be shown, with hurtful words being spoken on both sides. You may be up against an opponent who is equally matched to you, causing a stalemate. It is equally likely that you will have to take a far-reaching decision with little to guide you. This is not a time to allow your heart to rule your head. Only cool, calm logic will show the way forward.

## Reversed Meaning

Indecisiveness is shown when this card appears in the reversed position. Lack of foresight has landed you in trouble, and it could be hard to see which way to turn. So-called friends have offered little help, and may have added to the problem by betraying a confidence or giving the wrong advice. A malicious person may also be set to interfere, so proceed with caution!

# The Two of Pentacles or Diamonds

## Upright Meaning

Your finances may be rather depleted when this card appears in a reading. You will, however, cope with this quite well. Smart money-management is what you need, so start rescheduling and you will meet your obligations in full. You may have to take on extra work to get yourself out of difficulty, but this is certainly within your capabilities. In many cases, this card indicates the acquiring of new skills which will be useful to you in the future. It also promises that the cash-flow problem is temporary and ushers in a new, prosperous phase of your life.

## Reversed Meaning

In financial terms, the reversed two of Pentacles carries an unfortunate message. It foretells an unwise use of resources that may even result in insolvency. You could be living beyond your means, running up debts, and holding on to an unrealistic ideal. Equally, you may be moody and quite irritable because of an unspoken worry when this reversed card makes an appearance.

# Combinations

If one two card appears, there may be a period of confusion or stagnation. When three or four two cards are present, this can have the following special meanings (remember that the closer together the cards, the more important this subsidiary meaning is likely to be). Three twos indicate turbulent times, with many changes and much indecision. Four twos show that people will be gathering together for some special purpose; the reason for this could be revealed in the other cards. Note that two two cards have no additional significance in a reading.

# The Threes

In numerology, three equals success and natural growth. It is considered to be a masculine number, combining the initiative of one and the duality of two. Three is considered to be a "perfect" number, with religious connotations. Just think of how many trinities are found at the center of many of the world's faiths. Like the Empress of the Major Arcana (also numbered three), these Minor Arcana cards have associations with birth – the creation of new life, ideas, and projects that are often painful in the making.

## The Three of Rods or Clubs

### Upright Meaning
The three of Rods is a card of good fortune. It indicates a period of fast and furious activity. Letters, phone calls, good news, and many short journeys are to be expected in a period of increased opportunity. It may show that luck is on the way, and when you see this card in a reading you may be about to glimpse what is to come. Partnerships should prosper, too, in business and in your personal life, so the three of Rods is a good omen for marriage or the establishment of any close relationship.

### Reversed Meaning
Although the three of Rods is still a good card, even when reversed, it does tend to delay the good fortune that is foretold. It shows the need for patience, even though the card's fiery nature implies considerable impatience on your part. You may be overly proud and stubbornly independent at this time, refusing to face the reality of your present circumstances.

## The Three of Cups or Hearts

### Upright Meaning:
A time of celebration is foretold when the three of Cups appears in a reading. Fun and laughter are indicated here, as well as significant celebrations, such as a wedding, pregnancy, christening, or housewarming. You can be sure that you will attend a particularly enjoyable party. For some, the three of Cups is a prelude to a love affair, bringing lots of amorous action. This card also predicts that if there has been any ill-feeling in your life, the hurt will soon be healed.

### Reversed Meaning
The three of Cups has a promiscuous, or faithless, aspect when it is reversed. You may be taking the feelings of another person for granted, or you may be the victim of such treatment. There may be an illicit affair that is rapidly turning into an impossible love triangle. Perhaps you are about to be disappointed in love, and an affair close to your heart will end or become boringly static.

# The Three of Swords or Spades

## Upright Meaning
The three of Swords foretells pain. Loss and heartache are the key concepts of this unpleasant card. A relationship may come to a painful end, leaving you feeling hurt and bewildered. Sometimes the card indicates a sudden, upsetting shock that leaves you reeling. Illness or minor surgery may be shown, or at least a period of isolation and despondency. On a more positive note, this card irrevocably ends a situation. If that situation has, in itself, been testing for you, then it will soon be over as better times beckon.

## Reversed Meaning
There is little difference between the upright and reversed meanings of this card, yet in some ways the reversed three of Swords is more hopeful. Long-suffering heartache is coming to an end. The healing process has begun, so you will soon be feeling much better emotionally and physically. Try not to be impatient, though – take it slowly, as you still have some way to go.

# The Three of Pentacles or Diamonds

## Upright Meaning
The three of Pentacles often means buying or moving into a new home. Property issues are predominant here, so even if you are not moving, there will be work to do at your current address. The card has a positive meaning for other areas of your life, too. You will achieve an ambition that puts you head and shoulders above your colleagues and rivals. Although this may make others envious, there will be grudging respect for what you have accomplished. Let your talents shine, and make the most of all of the opportunities that come your way.

## Reversed Meaning
The envy indicated in the upright meaning is more evident when this card is reversed. However, this time you are the envious one. The card may also mean a waste of talent and a refusal to take the necessary steps to ensure your success. You may be too conservative in your attitudes, or merely content to dream about what you might do one day rather than actually make it happen.

# Combinations
The presence of only one of the threes in a reading can show a lack of energy, but if more than two of the three cards are grouped together in a reading, other, subsidiary interpretations come into play. The closer they are together, the more important these are likely to be. If there are three threes, the combination warns that you are being deceived and that you must take care when choosing those in whom you place your trust. If there are four threes, the emphasis is on determination and the ability to take action. You may be inspired by an idea and could be quite ruthless in putting it into practice. Note that two three cards have no additional significance in a reading.

# The Fours

In numerology, four is the number most associated with the earth, and the fours in the Minor Arcana therefore deal with practical affairs. The stability of the underlying Earth element is also reflected in the rather static nature of these cards. In essence, the fours represent a result achieved, and can either show a solid accomplishment or warn of the danger of getting into a rut.

## The Four of Rods or Clubs

### Upright Meaning

The four of Rods indicates a time of stability and establishment. It may indicate moving home, purchasing a new property, or, if not, an interior makeover. The card has many artistic associations and can reveal success and recognition in a creative sense – personal achievement is not far away, and this will have a positive and practical effect on your life. The four of Rods also indicates the successful completion of a project and the satisfaction of a job well done.

### Reversed Meaning

When this card is reversed, it suggests uncomfortable feelings of restriction. You may feel creatively frustrated, trapped in a boring job or in a place that you really don't want to be. This could, unfortunately, foster despondent feelings of inadequacy, and you may think that everything is pointless. In this position, the four of Rods delays outcomes, but take heart: your situation will improve as the upright meaning of the card eventually comes into play.

## The Four of Cups or Hearts

### Upright Meaning

There is a certain blindness associated with the four of Cups. It may be that you have a lot to be thankful for, with many advantages at your fingertips, but for some reason you cannot appreciate what you have achieved. You may feel that the grass is greener on the other side of the fence or that life is passing you by. Equally, when this card appears, you may not even know what you really want. In relationship matters, this card shows a need for some extra excitement, a renewal of the spark of romance before it fizzles out completely. You need new input to fuel your interest and rekindle your *joie de vivre*.

### Reversed Meaning

Although the meaning of this card does not really vary whether it is upright or reversed, in this position it reaches its extreme. Now there are only two choices: either you make a move, decide what you want, and go for it, or you shy away. You may fear loneliness or become overly hedonistic to stave off misery. Wake up, take positive action, and beat back this intense boredom!

# The Four of Swords or Spades

## Upright Meaning

The four of Swords is an indicator of illness, yet it is actually a good-news card. Hospitals, operations, and sickness are one interpretation, but you may not be the patient – and this card does, after all, promise recovery. In many ways, the appearance of the four of Swords can be welcomed as a chance to retreat from pressure and to make the most of a peaceful interlude to put your troubled thoughts in order. Even if a physical illness is not ailing you at the moment, take note of the four of Swords, because it reveals a desperate need to step back from stress. Remember that if you do not, this could be forced upon you.

## Reversed Meaning

The reversed meaning of the four is very similar to the upright meaning, but in this case it seems unlikely that life's stresses will be avoided. At the very least, this card indicates intense pressure and, if this is not alleviated, consequent depression. In this position, the need to take a break has become vital. Don't continue in this way: be kind to yourself, and rest accordingly.

# The Four of Pentacles or Diamonds

## Upright Meaning

This is one of the most steadfast cards in the Pentacles suit. It shows the achievement of financial stability, personal security, and the accumulation of possessions. More importantly, it shows that you will actually hang onto your gains, and that a period of worry will soon be over. You will soon find yourself in a comfortable situation. It's not just short-term benefits that are indicated here: you will do well in the long term, too. Savings schemes, property matters, insurance affairs, and anything concerning banks will work to your best advantage.

## Reversed Meaning

The reversed four of Pentacles has two distinct possibilities, so you will need to use your intuition to work out which one applies to you. On one hand, it can show miserliness and an uncompromising, grasping attitude. You may be envious of another's financial good fortune or be discontented with your own possessions. The other side of the coin, as it were, can show failure in tests and exams. Money may be short, and you could feel very insecure for a while.

## Combinations

When only one of the fours appears in a reading, it tends to signify a lack of balance and stability, while many fours clustered together can show a period of stagnation. However, if all four of these cards appear well spaced in a layout, then a time of contentment is more likely. If three appear together, then you can be sure that there's a lot of hard work ahead. Note that two four cards have no additional significance in a reading.

# The Fives

The number five has a strong symbolic association with the pentagram, the five-pointed star. In itself this is an ambiguous image. In paganism and magic, when upright (with one point facing upward), the star is thought to represent the four elements and the human soul, meaning order and rightness. In this position, the pentagram signifies the order of the universe and is sacred to pagans. However, when upside down, with the single point facing downward, the symbol represents disorder and chaos and has been seen as a graphic depiction of the devil's head. In the Tarot, the number five is linked to a transition that is often difficult, and possibly traumatic.

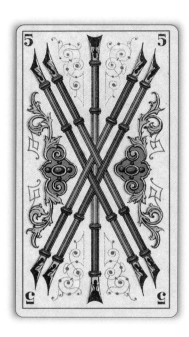

## The Five of Rods or Clubs

### Upright Meaning

The five of Rods presents a challenge. This is something that should get your pulse racing and raise your adrenaline levels. You may feel that you are not up to this test, or have momentary attacks of insecurity and anxiety. However, know that even if you feel nervous, you are perfectly capable of facing challenges and succeeding with a tremendous sense of accomplishment. You may have to overcome shyness to do this, asserting authority in a way that you have not attempted before. A subsidiary interpretation of this card involves dealing with contracts and written agreements.

### Reversed Meaning

There are misunderstandings aplenty when the five of Rods is reversed. Quarrels and bitter disputes may arise over petty matters, which at other, less stressful, moments would be ignored. You will be anxious and possibly feel inferior to others. Legal affairs cause worry, although they will not necessarily be unsuccessful. Do not be too trusting at this time.

## The Five of Cups or Hearts

### Upright Meaning

A time of emotional tension is forecast when the five of Cups appears in a reading. Fond affection has soured, bringing feelings of alienation and hostility. In many packs three cups remain standing, while two are overturned, spilling a bloodlike liquid. Indeed, there is the sense that something has been irrevocably lost and that emotionally things may never be quite the same again. However, the card has a more positive side, but it does present an emotional challenge of its own. You must stop fretting about what is past and turn your attention to what remains. This is your chance to leave a relationship that has given you little, or no, happiness, and strike out in a different direction.

### Reversed Meaning

There is still a sense of disappointment when this card is reversed, yet you will find that you will gain far more than you have lost. Again, the message is to stop dwelling on past failures and move on. The reversed five of Cups shows that your present unhappiness is transitory and will soon end.

# The Five of Swords or Spades

## Upright Meaning

The five of Swords shows that there are severe challenges to be met, but that it is unlikely that you will succeed. Defeat is almost certain, and it is best for you to acknowledge this and move on. Find a new path and don't let personal pride, ambition, or plain stubbornness dissuade you. You may have to make sacrifices, but it is better to start over than to cling to unrealistic ideals that will only bring you disappointment.

## Reversed Meaning

When reversed, the five of Swords unfortunately paints an even blacker picture than when in the upright position. There is a refusal to listen to reason and a stubborn persistence to continue to the bitter end – which, sadly, promises to be bitter indeed. Do yourself a favor when this five is negative: reconsider, hold back, and allow a project to runs its course – without you.

# The Five of Pentacles or Diamonds

## Upright Meaning

Poverty, or, at the very least, economic difficulties. The five of Pentacles points to a time of financial loss and of many obstacles to stability. You may feel somewhat excluded when this card appears in a reading. Doors that were once open to you will now be closed. On the other hand, you will not face these troubles alone. The card hints at a shared difficulty, and a mustering of resources may be needed to support you and a number of others in similar circumstances. This card can also suggest that you are looking for economic or emotional aid in the wrong places. Help and opportunities do exist, if only you can find them.

## Reversed Meaning

Loss is even greater when the five of Pentacles appears reversed, yet help will come to you in equal measure. It is probable that you have brought this crisis upon yourself and that now, being a little wiser, you may revise your attitude and set yourself back on a prosperous path. The going may be hard at first, yet this card does signify the first step toward an end to poverty.

# Combinations

Traditionally, it is said that to see only one five card in a reading is a good omen, showing that any problems will be insignificant. Two fives may show a delicate period, in which you will feel as if you are walking on eggshells. Three or four fives indicate an ongoing crisis that has reached a plateau, while all four grouped together indicate challenges, discord, and disputes.

# The Sixes

Six represents harmony in numerology. The cards to which this number relates have meanings reflecting kindness, charity, love, and beauty. When they are negative, they can show another aspect and can be fickle and flirtatious, promising much, yet delivering little. However, after the trials of the fours and fives, the sixes bring blessed relief and often indicate good times to come.

## The Six of Rods or Clubs

### Upright Meaning

Whereas the five of Rods brings challenges into your life, the six represents the aftermath of battle, and in this case, victory is yours. Now you will have the chance to take the time to enjoy your success, to reflect on the difficulties that you have faced, and to appreciate that you have overcome them. This card is also good for negotiating settlements, and, by extension, to any debate that you may embark upon. In legal affairs, this card is an excellent omen, again signifying a successful outcome. So whether the issue involves business advancement, a promotion, a negotiation, or any other related question, the answer of the six of Rods is victory.

### Reversed Meaning

Even when this card is reversed, the interpretation is positive, and you will achieve your desires. In this position, the six of Rods tends to delay matters, so perhaps you will get what is due to you – in time. Have patience and don't force an issue. It is better to let luck come to you, because you'll only waste your energy by pushing for results now.

## The Six of Cups or Hearts

### Upright Meaning

This is an extremely nostalgic card. In essence, the six of Cups relates to childhood and to the past in general. When this card appears in a reading, someone may come back into your life after a long absence. Happy memories are about to be reawakened, and certain past connections may resurface. Consider that the answer to a present problem may lie in past experience – so if you are facing a familiar situation now, your younger years may hold the key.

### Reversed Meaning

When reversed, the six of Cups is a little too sugary for your own good. A rose-tinted view of the past may be obscuring the truth. You may be being held back by old ideas and the imagined disapproval of childhood role models. This card could be a message to grow up and take a more adult stance, make your own decisions and not allow the past to rule your life.

# The Six of Swords or Spades

## Upright Meaning
Even though Sword cards usually mean trouble, thankfully the six of Swords means getting away from it. The appearance of this card in a reading suggests an escape from immediate difficulties and generally moving into a happier, more productive, phase. Physical travel is often associated with this card, and a well-deserved vacation after a time of intense stress is the traditional interpretation. A change of scene will boost your morale and remind you that the world isn't always a place of struggle. The six of Swords heralds the end of a trying time.

## Reversed Meaning
The troubles indicated by this upright Sword card will continue for a while longer, but there is now hope, and you should be feeling more positive about your prospects. Exert just a little more effort and you will soon move forward. Stay determined – you are not yet in the clear, but take heart that calmer days are coming.

# The Six of Pentacles or Diamonds

## Upright Meaning
This is a very philanthropic card. The six of Pentacles suggests that you will receive a gift that will help your financial position enormously. You may receive a windfall payment, some unearned cash, or a present that will be very precious to you on a personal level. You could benefit from an investment or a trust fund, or even an unexpected inheritance. Even if the help that you get doesn't come in the form of money, it will be of great practical assistance. Traditionally, this is the card of patronage, of receiving support when you need it most. Remember to be suitably grateful to your benefactor!

## Reversed Meaning
Extravagant spending could be at the root of your problems just now. In common with some other reversed Pentacle cards, such as the five and eight, the six warns against living beyond your means, running up debts, and generally being irresponsible with cash. It also has connections with financial settlements, such as alimony, wills, and dissolving a business partnership. You may also find that something has to be shared out, such as furniture or other belongings. Continuing the somber message, take extra care of your own possessions now, as opportunists may strike.

# Combinations
The harmonious nature of the number six ensures that the appearance of a six in your reading is a good omen. Two sixes show a certain resignation on your part concerning a future event, and this attitude could be either positive or negative. Three sixes grouped closely together show an active social life, lots of fun, and rapport with your friends, while four sixes show situations that can be turned to your advantage, even if this is not immediately obvious.

# The Sevens

Seven was traditionally considered to be one of the "perfect numbers," being the combination of the dynamic number three and the stable four. It was also thought to be special because it is a prime number, divisible only by itself and one. From the days of the week to the colors of the rainbow, seven has many connections with mythology, astrology, and symbolism. Until the late eighteenth century, astronomers held that there were seven known planets; the Great Bear constellation, dominating the Northern sky, has seven stars. In alchemy, there were said to be seven stages in the quest for the Philosopher's Stone, and, of course, there are said to be seven heavens. Some of this magical thinking is reflected in the interpretations of the sevens of the Minor Arcana.

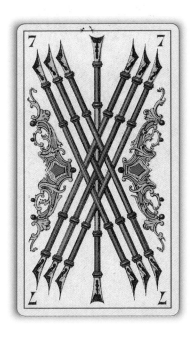

## The Seven of Rods or Clubs

### Upright Meaning

The seven of Rods places a barrier in your path. However, this is not a card to bring you to a dead stop. You have plenty of energy and should now test your wits. In the past, you may have come up against opposition, and, if so, it is vital that you now stand your ground and be assertive. Only firm belief will enable you to conquer the challenge. There may be more than one problem plaguing you, but be methodical and deal with each in turn. Be brave":you've faced worse troubles in the past.

### Reversed Meaning

Self-doubt is your greatest enemy when the seven of Rods is reversed. Your timidity could defeat you, even when the outlook is good, so believe in yourself and in your abilities. An unusual situation could arise that could worry and possibly embarrass you in the future unless you nip it in the bud at once.

# The Seven of Cups or Hearts

## Upright Meaning

The seven of Cups is a card about confusion. There are just too many choices to be made at once and too many people to listen to, each of whom has a different perspective. The only way to deal with this is to trust in your instincts. Disregard all of this well-meaning advice and just go with the option that feels right. It is true that all is not as it seems, but no amount of logic will sort the true from the false in these circumstances. There are truly amazing opportunities around, so be sure to make the most of them. Aside from all of this decision-making, if a romance has been beset by a lack of funds, this will soon be resolved.

## Reversed Meaning

The message of the seven of Cups reversed is the same as the upright meaning, but you must take extra care. The wrong decision is easy to make at the moment, and your wishful thinking may be leading you astray.

# The Seven of Swords or Spades

## Upright Meaning

This is quite a difficult card to interpret. Because it can indicate a theft or fraud in your future, it is time to take extra care of your possessions. On the other hand, this card can be an indicator that someone has been "robbed" of confidence by a faithless lover or false friend. Lies and intrigue are around you and you will need all of your cunning to match an opponent. However, your efforts may not be wholehearted and you may have to make a sacrifice in order to succeed at this difficult time. Legal affairs and business dealings may not prosper when the seven of Swords appears.

## Reversed Meaning

The significance of the reversed seven of Swords is even more unhappy than the upright meaning. It makes theft, lies, and general dishonesty far more likely, with the added complication of malice. Be very wary of whom you trust, and don't take anything at face value when you see this card reversed. It might be a good idea to triple-check your home security.

# The Seven of Pentacles or Diamonds

## Upright Meaning

This card may be fortunate, but it cannot be described as exciting. A slow, but sure, progression toward your goal is the interpretation of the upright seven of Pentacles. This is therefore a card of hard work and unremitting effort. You will attain your longed-for rewards, but you have to keep at it. This card usually appears when a job simply becomes too tedious to be borne, yet the message of the card is that you are on the right track, so don't give up. It also encourages forward-planning. Perseverance is the key to your success.

## Reversed Meaning:

As might be expected, the reversed seven of Pentacles is about idleness, wasting time and energy, and generally feeling that you would very much like to have all of the rewards now, without the tedious business of putting in all of that effort. Unfair as it may seem, there is no substitute for hard work just now.

# Combinations

One, two, or three sevens in a reading is considered a good omen. All are considered dynamic and positive forces. Two sevens in close proximity are said to denote true love. The sevens bring business success and partnership cooperation. However, all four together tip the balance and warn of intrigue, lies, and the possibility of theft.

# The Eights

In numerology, eight denotes structure, harmony, and balance. In the Tarot, the number is also associated with the concept of progress, so it is not surprising that the four eights generally refer to movement. The most speedy example of this is found in the suit of Rods, and the least active in the challenging suit of Swords. Eight is also said to be the number of karma, which means that you are rewarded or chastized for past actions, so these cards also reflect a degree of moral judgement.

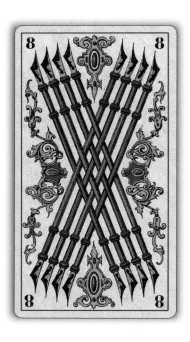

## The Eight of Rods or Clubs

### Upright Meaning

Things are about to pick up their pace when the eight of Rods is upright in your reading. The card is associated with speed, so you will need to think on your feet. You will be receiving more phone calls, e-mails, and faxes than usual, your mailbox will be full to bursting, and you'll have but a short time to get everything done. Travel is more likely when this card turns up, but because this is a Rod card, your journey may have more to do with business than with pleasure, although you'll probably have fun along the way. Traditionally, this card speeds up other events that are revealed in the rest of the reading.

### Reversed Meaning

In a total reversal of the upright meaning, the eight of Rods inverted is very frustrating, forecasting delays, unexpected complications, and lots of missed phone calls. People whom you need to see may not be available just now, and your impatience may get the better of you. You may even be overly hasty or rude to someone whom you really should not offend. This is not a good time to put down your thoughts in writing.

# The Eight of Cups or Hearts

## Upright Meaning

An emotional break with the past is forecast when the eight of Cups is found in a spread. It's time to move on, to experience the new, and to spread your wings a little. This card is an omen of pleasurable travel, because now you can see more of the world and learn more about yourself in the process. If you have been caught up in petty worries and other people's problems, take heart, because a new path to a brighter future beckons. Of course, this journey may not actually be a physical one, but may indicate that you have traveled a long way in a spiritual sense. Either way, the essential message is the same: take notice of your deepest desires and follow your heart. Who knows what you may find?

## Reversed Meaning

You could be running away from your problems rather than making the effort to solve them when this card is reversed. You may even be in pursuit of an unreal dream at the expense of what is good and solid in your life. The reversed eight of Cups warns that you are likely to be making a far-reaching error of judgement. Take care!

# The Eight of Swords or Spades

## Upright Meaning

True to form for the suit of Swords, the eight suggests a run of bad luck. You may feel that you are trapped by circumstances, with no possibility of escaping a dreadful turn of events. It is certain that panicking will not help, and that only patient effort will get you out of this situation. However, there is a positive aspect to this card: it shows that help is available to you if you know where to find it. Think hard, because there is someone who could come to your aid. Perhaps it is simply pride that is standing in your way. Be sensible and ask!

## Reversed Meaning

When the eight of Swords is reversed, the frustration that you are feeling at a difficult time can be almost unbearable. You may be irritable and prone to taking your negative feelings out on others. In this case, you are likely to be your own worst enemy, refusing to see that the way out is perfectly obvious and that you are unwilling to do anything about it. As with the upright position, pride may be the root cause of the problem.

# The Eight of Pentacles or Diamonds

## Upright Meaning

A period of learning is about to begin when the eight of Pentacles appears in your spread. For many, this will be the beginning of an educational phase, for others a new job, in which new skills will be developed. The card suggests patient effort in pursuit of a worthwhile, long-term goal. You may be adding to your qualifications or just taking a hobby or interest that one step farther. It is certain that the skills that you learn now will be of immense benefit to you in the future, so work hard and you will receive ample reward.

## Reversed Meaning

When the eight of Pentacles is reversed, there is a desire for a "quick fix." You will be impatient, forget your future aims, and desire all of the rewards now! You may be distracted from work by personal problems, or, conversely, by having too much of a good time. Your performance may suffer and your standards drop as you seem content to settle for second best. At worst, this card suggests the loss of a lucrative job.

# Combinations

If a solitary eight occurs in your reading, then there will be a certain lack of harmony in your life. (If this is the eight of Swords, then this will be particularly apparent.) Two eights bring surprises of all kinds and provide physical energy. Three eights may suggest good news, especially in connection with your relationships, while all four eights appearing together make travel more certain.

# The Nines

In numerology, the number nine is the third of the "perfect numbers." If considered as three times three, it symbolizes the beginning and the end. It is said to be the most selfish of numbers, too, because no matter how many times one multiplies it, nine will always return to itself: 9 x 2 = 18, 1 + 8 = 9, 3 x 9 = 27, 2+7 = 9, and so on. In the Tarot, the number is seen as extremely complex, and may be said to embody the perfected essence of each suit. The nine of Rods is a steady flame, the nine of Cups a gushing fountain, the nine of Swords is one of the most troubled cards in a troubled suit, and the nine of Pentacles is complete material comfort.

## The Nine of Rods or Clubs

### Upright Meaning
Hard work appears to be at an end when the nine of Rods appears in the upright position. However, it's not over yet – it's just that you don't seem to be going anywhere just now. You have achieved stability and great self-confidence, and know that you can deal with anything that the world throws at you. If you are having a stressful time, the appearance of the nine of Rods is extremely reassuring, promising that if you stand your ground just a little longer, you will gain complete victory. Be patient, and maintain your position while remaining vigilant. This card proves the virtues of patience.

### Reversed Meaning
When the nine of Rods is reversed, the virtuous stability of the upright card now becomes stifling. You may refuse to compromise in a dispute that could be resolved easily if only you were more flexible. Your opinions are misguided, but if challenged, you'll cling to your beliefs even more obstinately.

# The Nine of Cups or Hearts

## Upright Meaning
The joyful nature of the Cup cards reaches a pinnacle in the nine. Happiness and fun are all around you, for this card is an excellent omen for your social life. It foretells parties, social gatherings, and places of entertainment. New people will come into your life and you will make many new friends. The card also suggests improvements in health and a more positive mental attitude. Your relationships will be more fulfilling, your popularity more evident, and your sense of fun more infectious. The nine of Cups boosts communication and lets you open your heart and mind to new and exciting ideas.

## Reversed Meaning
When the nine of Cups is negatively placed, the worst side of this suit comes into play. Vanity, arrogance, and taking the feelings of others for granted are the less attractive aspects that may be expressed. Your partner and close friends may feel neglected as you become increasingly fickle and self-absorbed. Conversely, you may be being overly sentimental, cloying, and possessive.

# The Nine of Swords or Spades

## Upright Meaning

There's no getting away from that fact that the nine of Swords is simply dreadful! When this card appears in a reading, it is an omen of sleepless nights, anxiety, and feelings of powerlessness. You may be a victim of spite and, although you may struggle against it, this could leave you feeling undermined. You may be feeling guilty, enduring a form of self-punishment of some sort. Illness is a traditional meaning of the card, suggesting that you will need much determination to see you through treatment and recuperation. Female health issues are also indicated by the nine of Swords.

## Reversed Meaning

The interpretation of the reversed card is little different from the upright version. However, it does make self- punishment more likely. You may even refuse help through false pride or simply because you think that your situation is hopeless. The opposite is the case though, because when the card is reversed there is light at the end of the tunnel, even if you cannot see it yet.

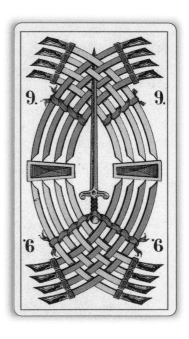

# The Nine of Pentacles or Diamonds

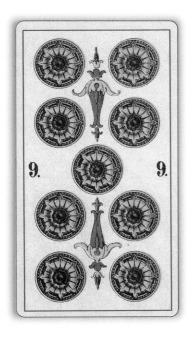

## Upright Meaning

Comfort and the enjoyment of the good things of life are the basic interpretations of the nine of Pentacles. This card shows prosperity, the exercise of good sense and excellent taste, as well as the benefits of financial shrewdness. When this card appears, you will soon be able to congratulate yourself on a job well done, step back from your everyday concerns, and reward yourself for all of your labors. You can now afford to relax a little. Traditionally, the card means that you'll have the leisure time to enjoy the ambience of your home and take pleasure in your garden. It can also suggest buying new furniture and generally spoiling yourself.

## Reversed Meaning

When negative, this card warns of living beyond your means, treating your resources in a cavalier fashion, accruing heavy debts, and generally being irresponsible with both your own and others' funds. It may suggest success that is founded on the misfortunes of others. There could also be a danger of theft or fraud, so keep your wits about you and be especially careful with your possessions.

# Combinations

When only one nine appears in a reading, it shows that even if you have problems you will keep them under control. If two appear close together, then you will soon be dealing with legal documents and contracts. Three nines foretell prosperity and good health (even if one of them happens to be the nine of Swords), while all four together show that you will overcome all difficulties and be rewarded with recognition for your accomplishments.

# The Tens

According to the rules of numerology, when we reach the number ten, symbolically we are returning to one (1 + 0 =1). Therefore the elemental qualities of the aces are again in evidence, but this time expressed on a higher plane. The ancient Greek philosophers saw the number as holding all other numbers within it, so they identified it with divinity. The tens can be regarded as the ultimate of their suit.

The potential associated with the one cards of the suits has now been fulfilled, and another set of circumstances now exists. When a ten appears in a reading the end of a cycle has been reached for good or ill, because it symbolizes the completion of journeys and the return to origins. Ten has many symbolic associations, such as the Ten Commandments of the Old Testament and the ten spheres on the cabbalistic Tree of Life in Hebrew mysticism.

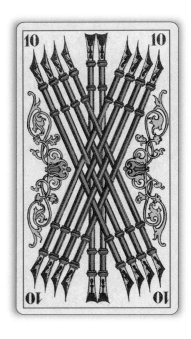

## The Ten of Rods or Clubs

### Upright Meaning

Because Rods generally speak of creation and those things that require effort, the ten of Rods foretells a period of great pressure, of hard work, and the acceptance of duty. You may be shouldering burdens, be engaged in the completion of an arduous task, or feel that you are under considerable stress. You will know that a worthwhile project must be carried through to the very end, and will have all of the determination and personal resources you need to carry out this obligation. However, even though the price may be high in terms of your stress and anxiety levels, the card does promise astounding success as a reward for your mammoth efforts. You may also have to prioritize and defer less important duties to make time for the vital task in hand.

### Reversed Meaning

There is little difference from the upright in the reversed meaning of the card. However, in this case, others may be placing unnecessary pressure on you, which you will feel duty-bound to accept. There may be other agendas at play, and people may take advantage of you, possibly disrupting your plans.

## The Ten of Cups or Hearts

### Upright Meaning

The passionate or turbulent emotions of the early Cup cards have mellowed into a feeling of perfect contentment when we reach the ten of Cups. Peace and prosperity are promised by this card, which fills your life with joy. You can be sure that the happiness that is foretold by the Cups ten is going to last. Peace and harmony are keywords here, friendships will flourish, and closer relationships will become even more satisfying. This is an excellent indicator of pleasurable group activities that will bring a lot of fun back into your life. It may indicate that a wish will be fulfilled and that everything will work out in the best possible way. The card also has strong associations with family life, which will be extremely fulfilling.

### Reversed Meaning

Even when reversed, this card cannot really be a bad one. However, you may be mistrustful of your good fortune, and your past experience may be urging you toward cynicism. Even so, the outlook is still good. Some friends may leave your circle, and you may feel somewhat isolated for a short while. Even so, nature abhors a vacuum, and others will soon come to replace those who are gone.

# The Ten of Swords or Spades

## Upright Meaning

As the ultimate card of a difficult suit, the ten of Swords has the reputation of being the worst card in the deck. It speaks of being left in the cold or betrayed – metaphorically stabbed in the back. One of its traditional names is "ruin." When this card turns up, all that you dread is likely to occur. However, when things become so bad that they can't possibly get any worse, there is only one way to go, and that's up! Looked at another way, the ten of Swords reveals that a run of bad luck can't possibly continue forever. After all, when all is lost, what more is there to lose? This is the turning point, when a glimmer of good fortune will give you cause for hope. Slowly your confidence will be restored and you will eventually turn away from the unpleasantness that has dogged you for so long.

## Reversed Meaning

The upright meaning of this card holds true, even when it is reversed, but it also means that you haven't reached rock bottom quite yet. There may be one more stroke of bad luck to come before the turning point. At this time, it is important to be positive and to bolster your ego in any way you know how. Don't give into despair.

# The Ten of Pentacles or Diamonds

## Upright Meaning

As the ultimate expression of the materialistic suit of Pentacles, the ten means wealth. Of course, there is more than one kind of wealth, although if you find this card in your reading it is a pretty good indicator that your financial fortunes will improve considerably. The card relates to family life and shows harmony between generations, too. There is also a sense of handing on property or money by means of gifts or even an inheritance. Tradition comes within this card's influence, so one interpretation is carrying on the customs of the past. The ten of Pentacles is also one of the indicators of marriage, and if that's what you have in mind, then a prosperous and happy future is in store.

## Reversed Meaning

There may be family disputes when the ten of Pentacles is reversed. Quarrels over money or inheritance rights are all too likely, yet right will win over all opposition eventually, even if you have to go through something of an emotional mill to get there. The good traditions associated with the upright card take on a negative interpretation here, although on a positive note, it may be that old ways of thinking and of doing things are stifling originality.

# Combinations

When a single ten appears in a spread, significant changes are on the way that will change your life. Two tens may indicate new employment and a stroke of good luck (if one of these is the ten of Swords, this luck may not be immediately obvious). Three tens bring legal or contractual difficulties, while all four together bring great changes that are all to the good (even if they appear to be dreadful at first) and remarkable triumphs. However, if any are reversed, then there are still obstacles to overcome.

FANTE DI BASTONI

# The Page of Rods or Clubs

## Description
A child or young person of either sex, with blue or hazel eyes, brown hair, and a ruddy complexion. He or she tends to be talkative, even loud, and certainly impossible to ignore.

## Upright Meaning
The young person described by the page of Rods is very enthusiastic, adaptable, and hard-working. He or she is willing, even anxious, to please; this youth may be a traveler or someone who brings you a surprising message. Their down side, however, is impatience, impulsiveness, and hyperactivity – constantly on the move, these pages are easily bored and have little staying power. On the other hand, you will never, ever be bored in their company. After all, there is charm here, and although voluble, he or she always has plenty of interesting things to say.

## Reversed Meaning
A rather spoiled individual is revealed when this card is reversed. This page likes his or her own way and will constantly demand attention. The card may show a faithless lover, a person who has a long list of complaints, and someone who brings bad news. Lack of application is this young person's problem. In some cases, there may be educational problems, such as difficulty with reading or writing.

## Possible Events
When this card appears as an "event" card, it generally means messages from all directions. Phone calls, mail, and faxes need your attention. It also urges you carefully to consider your next move, even if your instincts demand that you take instant action. Perhaps there is an important fact that you are missing. The page can also suggest a reunion with an old friend.

FANTE DI BASTONI

# The Page of Cups or Hearts

## Description

A blond, blue-eyed youngster of either sex, usually rather pale-skinned. This child will be dreamy, often with a far-away look and a soft voice. Very loving, this person looks for emotional security and approval.

## Upright Meaning

This page is gentle and caring, and possibly quite insecure. He or she has artistic gifts and may be intuitive and insightful. If the card describes a girl, then she is tomboyish in behavior, if a boy, then somewhat feminine. Whatever gender the page happens to be, this is someone who is emotionally vulnerable and who needs reassurance. There is also a Peter Pan quality here, so bear in mind that this card does not always describe a particularly young person. The page of Cups can be any age, but with an extremely youthful outlook.

FANTE DI COPPE

## Reversed Meaning

When reversed, the page of Cups is rather trivial and spoiled. This is someone who exaggerates their own weaknesses to play on the sympathies of others. He or she is petulant, demands the impossible, and is then difficult to deal with when thwarted. If the dream world of this page is challenged, they tend to become very angry when reality does not match up to the fantasy.

## Possible Events

It could be too easy to fall head over heels in love when this page appears as an "event" card. However, it is not a good idea to give your heart so readily. Try to be more logical and listen to a friend's advice. The object of your desire may not be all that he or she seems. Another interpretation involves the need to study for exams.

# The Page of Swords or Spades

## Description
A young person of either sex, with dark hair and penetrating eyes. Like other Sword court cards, this youngster usually has pale skin and sharply defined features.

## Upright Meaning
Intelligence and swift perception are the hallmarks of the page of Swords. Very little gets past him or her, and it is unwise to try to fool them in any way. Like other Sword court cards, the page has eloquence and can wield this gift like a weapon, occasionally becoming sarcastic. However, he or she is eager to learn and is extremely skilled at turning apparent misfortunes to their advantage. This is a good person to have on your side, because the page makes a fantastic ally. The page of Swords may bring you into contact with helpful people and provide good news.

## Reversed Meaning
There is an aura of danger about the reversed page of Swords. This knave is a spy or a rival, a slanderer, a sneak, and a formidable opponent. No trick is too underhand or too dirty, so take care when dealing with him or her. The reversed page is rarely open about feelings, so you rarely will you know where you stand. Old bitterness for imagined wrongs has turned into spite, and this could be expressed as subtle malice and calculated lies.

## Possible Events
Be as cool as you possibly can. There are hidden dangers, so you will need to keep your wits about you. You may be the victim of slander and malice, but do not take action yet. These are early days, and your enemies could make a big mistake and undo their own plans. Legal disputes may be indicated.

# The Page of Pentacles or Diamonds

## Description
A young person of either sex, with a tanned or dark complexion, dark-brown or black hair, and a ready smile. This youngster may be rather introverted and longs to be appreciated.

## Upright Meaning
The page of Pentacles is a conscientious young person, who is older than his or her years. There is a capacity for hard work and thrift, a necessity because of a lack of money. However, the page is only just starting out in life and has splendid prospects. How could he or she fail with such a strong sense of duty, right and wrong, and the value of labor? The card could represent a student or an apprentice – one who is working not for immediate gains, but for a worthy cause or ambition.

FANTE DI DANARI

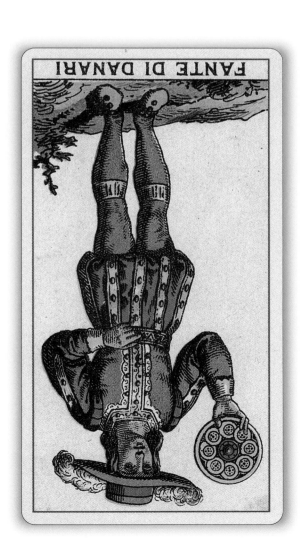

## Reversed Meaning
The reversed page of Pentacles is the complete opposite of its upright equivalent. This page is a bit of a scoundrel, who drains your resources faster than you can gain them. He or she has a constant need for money and has cunning ways of gaining it. Of course, working for it is something that this rogue is most reluctant to do. A lack of foresight and total impatience are the main traits of the reversed page of Pentacles.

## Possible Events
Like other Pentacles cards, the page relates to money, which indicates that there's a shortage. A step-by-step, methodical approach to the problem will eventually solve the cash-flow crisis, but get-rich-quick schemes will only make matters worse. Be prudent and take careful steps. On a positive note, any money news will be good.

## Combinations
Four pages grouped together in a reading suggest colleges, universities, and anywhere that young people gather. Three pages show the prospect of an excellent social life, no matter what your age, while two pages often denote petty arguments between friends. This is especially true if the page of Rods and the page of Cups turn up, because these two are traditionally thought of as enemies simply because their natures are so contrary. Note that a single page in a reading has no additional significance, other than its divinatory meaning.

CAVAL. DI BASTONI

# The Knight of Rods or Clubs

## Description
A vigorous, active young man, who tends to have an athletic build and a ruddy complexion. Since this is a Fiery suit, this Knight may give the impression of haste, often jumping to conclusions.

## Upright Meaning
The knight of Rods represents a traveler or a visitor from afar. It is likely that he has faced many challenges and has overcome them with the courage of a born warrior. This knight is generous, but he does tend to be hasty, so if you don't impress him within the first couple of seconds it's unlikely that you'll get a second chance. However, his innate good humor should get you through this. The knight of Rods proves a worthwhile friend and a firm ally.

## Reversed Meaning
When in the reversed position, the knight of Rods is extremely argumentative. His fiery nature forces him into confrontations with others, even when these are totally unnecessary. He seems to thrive on rivalry and open conflict. He may even possess a violent streak, which stems from bitter jealousy. His word, although given in absolute sincerity, can prove worthless.

## Possible Events
If the knight of Rods does not represent a person in your reading, then it is likely that you will soon be moving home. A sudden, brilliant idea may occur that will start you off on a brand-new path. If the card is reversed, then you may be burning your bridges in some way – for good or ill.

CAVAL. DI BASTONI

# The Knight of Cups or Hearts

## Description

A young man, with fair skin and hair, casual in dress, and possessing a slightly bohemian air. Often well traveled, he will be aware of fashion and culture in other parts of the world.

## Upright Meaning

The arrival of the knight of Cups in a reading suggests that you are about to meet a new lover or a good friend. His character is noted for enthusiasm, passion, and amiability. He may be artistically gifted, poetic, and graceful. He has an empathy with the feelings of others, and is a sympathetic and understanding ally. This is good news, because this card shows that changes in your relationships are now in the offing. These may worry you, yet all will turn out for the best if this knight has anything to do with it. Often the card occurs when offers and opportunities of an emotional nature are on their way.

## Reversed Meaning

When the knight of Cups is reversed, a lover will soon depart. This is likely to be a good thing since the character of this reversed knight is not an attractive one, even though the card is associated with good looks. This personality is virtually immoral, a swindler and a faithless lover leaving a trail of broken hearts in his wake. Face it: you are better off without him in your life.

## Possible Events

If this knight does not seem to be a particular person in your reading, then sudden changes in your emotional state are to be expected. Instant attractions and the beginning of amorous relationships are indicated. If reversed, your feelings may be abused by a fickle lover.

CAVAL. DI SPADE

# The Knight of Swords or Spades

## Description
This card describes a tall, dark man. This knight possesses much charm, wit, and perception. Often eccentric in his mode of dress, he rarely has much patience with convention.

## Upright Meaning
The courage of the knight of Swords is beyond question. He is a brave, tough, intelligent young man, with the gift of eloquence. He is charming and attractive, one who will suddenly hurl himself into your life and, like the wind, may blow out again just as quickly. His intelligence ensures that he needs lots of stimulation to hold his interest, as he tends to become bored very easily. The same cannot be said of any dealings with him: he is quite impetuous, so his adventures, and the tales that he tells of them, will rarely cause boredom in others.

## Reversed Meaning
The impetuosity of the upright knight of Swords becomes something of a nightmare when the card is reversed. This character has no staying power at all and is constantly getting into trouble. He may be violent, he is certainly secretive and treacherous, and, although immensely plausible, he will tell the most outrageous lies to suit his purposes. His intelligence makes it very difficult for anyone to catch him out.

## Possible Events
If the knight of Swords does not represent a person in your reading, then a whirlwind of events will confuse you as circumstances suddenly change and other people's attitudes become unpredictable. If reversed, there are battles to be fought, so prepare for conflict.

CAVAL. DI SPADE

# The Knight of Pentacles or Diamonds

## Description
A dark-skinned, swarthy young man, with a good income. He is generally discreet, conservative in his clothes and in his lifestyle. This knight often has very dark hair and eyes.

## Upright Meaning
Caution is the watchword of the knight of Pentacles. It has been said that he rides not a charger but a carthorse. It may be slow, but he is sure to get where he wants to go! This character is analytical, leaving little to chance. He is extremely practical and a hard worker. He accepts responsibility easily, is a steadfast and trustworthy person, and, although he may seem quiet and reserved at first, he has hidden depths. Apart from his ambition, which is strong, there are also earthy, physical passions around that might come as a shock to those who do not know him well.

## Reversed Meaning
The steadfastness of the upright knight of Pentacles turns into mind-numbing boredom when the card is reversed. This knight is not slow: he is static; unimaginative, mean, and petty-minded. Conversely, the knight may represent a person who comes up with a scheme to make money. However, you will find that if you agree to it, it's going to cost you lots. This knight is dull-witted, smug, and careless, or, if not, then timid to the point of cowardice.

## Possible Events
Fairly rapid economic development is the likely interpretation of this card if it does not seem to represent a person in your reading. You are bound to benefit from these financial changes, but be patient. If the card is reversed, it may show sudden reversals of fortune, but these will be temporary.

## Combinations
There will be little room for pause or reflection when a number of knights appears in a spread. All four grouped together indicate speedy action, breathtaking events that might scare you somewhat, rapid developments, and probable sudden travel. Three knights indicate small gatherings of men (if any are reversed, there will be a troublemaker among them). Two knights usually mean reunions with old friends, but if the knights of Cups and Rods appear close to each other, beware, because these are rivals in love. Note that one knight in a reading has no additional significance, other than its own divinatory meaning.

# The Queen of Rods or Clubs

REGINA DI BASTONI

## Description

The queen of Rods is a woman of dignity, with a passionate or fiery temperament. Her coloring tends to be fair, with blue or hazel eyes. Her hair is any shade darker than blond, and is in many cases reddish.

## Upright Meaning

The queen of Rods is a lady with an independent and passionate nature. She is freedom-loving, lively, and often creatively gifted. She may run a business or be employed in an administrative position. Warm-hearted and tender, she combines these admirable traits with practicality. Noted as an organizer of others, the queen of Rods is well liked, as her influence is a powerful force for good. She is a willing helper, on condition that those whom she helps will eventually stand on their own feet. Traditionally, she is said to prefer the countryside to the town and to appreciate the diversity of nature.

## Reversed Meaning

Mean and possessive, the reversed queen of Rods is not a person to cross. She can be dictatorial, vengeful, and vindictive, hating independence of thought or action in others. Jealousy and ill-temper are the negative traits of her fiery nature. Her passion is often thwarted, leading to even more unpleasant expressions of bad feeling.

## Possible Events

When the queen of Rods appears as an "event" card, then it warns against relying too heavily on others. You may be somewhat introverted and need to get about more. If the card is reversed, then this shyness may be hampering your ability to communicate.

# The Queen of Cups or Hearts

REGINA DI COPPE

## Description

The queen of Cups symbolizes a beautiful woman, with expressive, liquid blue eyes and a very fair complexion. This lady turns heads wherever she goes, expressing a physical sensuality that is evident in her movements.

## Upright Meaning

Dreamy and poetic, the queen of Cups is a lover of dancing, music, and of love itself. She has a great capacity for imagination and artistic gifts that should be encouraged, because, being such an emotional soul, she may too easily lose heart in overly critical company. This queen is sympathetic and sociable, with time for everyone. She is honest, loyal, and caring, with a sweet character and a charitable disposition. She follows her heart and creates harmony and happiness wherever she goes. As the queen of Cups is instinctively in tune with the deeper feelings of those around her, she must choose her companions carefully.

## Reversed Meaning

This lover of life can become immoral and vain when the card is reversed. She may be deceitful and perverse, forcing others to indulge her idle whims and constantly demanding their attention. This person may be spoiled and impervious to reason, seeing no higher value than her own desires. She may be a faithless lover or a woman who is content to drain the financial and emotional resources of those close to her.

## Possible Events

This deeply emotional card shows that issues of the heart predominate in your life. You may want to show the object of your desire the extent of your love or to express your creative gifts in a more productive way. If reversed, this card shows that you are not thinking logically enough.

REGINA DI SPADE

# The Queen of Swords or Spades

## Description

The queen of Swords is usually pale-skinned, with thin lips and dark hair. Her eyes may be dark, or shades of gray, blue, or green. No matter what her age, she expresses a maturity of attitude and has a good line in disapproving looks. Her build is slight and she may be quite tall.

## Upright Meaning

First and foremost, the queen of Swords is an extremely independent person. Like the king of the same suit, she is highly intelligent, prefers the world of the mind, is logical, and approaches every problem and crisis with cool rationale. Noted for her physical grace, this queen is fond of music and dancing, loves reading, and hates wasting time. Little gets past her keen perception. She is very alert to the undercurrents in the lives of those around her, and her intuition and brain power should not be underestimated. Traditionally, this card is said to represent a widow or divorcee.

## Reversed Meaning

Jealousy and malice are the best descriptors of the reversed queen of Swords. She may be bitter because of past hurt and, as a result, is a harsh critic of others' actions and particularly of their morals. In some cases, the reversed queen is prudish, or at least lives by a set of rules that are so inflexible that no one could possibly live up to them. If she acts as a go-between, she stirs up plenty of trouble through her half-truths and outright lies.

## Possible Events

Deep concentration and focusing upon your goal will overcome any obstacles. However, the card's notorious reputation comes into its own when the queen of Swords is reversed. Then it shows insincerity, scheming, and interference. If this is you just now, you may be being too manipulative for your own good, and you will be found out.

# The Queen of Pentacles or Diamonds

## Description

The queen of Pentacles may be thought of as a motherly type of woman. Tradition states that she tends to be of a large build, with a strong constitution and a cheerful face. Like other Pentacles court cards, her coloring tends to be dark, with large, expressive, dark eyes.

## Upright Meaning

The queen of Pentacles represents a sensible, down-to-earth woman, with a good head for business and in particular an excellent way of handling finances. This is the sort of person who has to handle many jobs at once in both the professional and domestic spheres. On the other hand, this queen has a taste for the good life, too. She knows how to enjoy herself, and her good humor is infectious. Obviously she is very caring, but no one will blame her for being moody now and again.

## Reversed Meaning

A selfish, miserly, and greedy woman, who loathes change and is suspicious of everyone around her. She may perceive her own family members to be as grasping as she is and causes discord wherever she goes. Another interpretation of these traits would be a woman who will literally do anything for money. Yet another might be someone who is very poor, but does not bear her misfortune with good grace.

## Possible Events

Too much anxiety over financial matters, or being too protective of others. The motherly nature of the card may cause unnecessary worry over the lives of one's children or other dependants. If the card is reversed, however, these worries may have something more to them, so do investigate.

## Combinations

When all four queens appear close together in a reading, then small gatherings of women are about to become a feature of your life. However, if these cards are reversed, then gossip and carping complaints may spoil the event and make you feel inferior in some way. Three queens symbolize helpful female friends, while two queens are a bad sign, signifying barely concealed rivalries and treachery. Note that a solo queen in a reading has no additional significance, other than its divinatory meaning.

# The King of Rods or Clubs

RE DI BASTONI

## Description

The king of Rods is a person of maturity who exhibits great authority. He is probably of athletic build, healthy, and vigorous. He is also likely to be brown-haired, with hazel or blue eyes.

## Upright Meaning

A worldly-wise, successful, professional man. He is someone who is likely to have traveled a great deal. He may be a businessman or employed in a managerial capacity. This king is quite old-fashioned in the best sense – gentlemanly, just, and honorable. He is noted for his kindness and generosity (which may just be an excuse to show off), and makes an excellent and unbiased advisor. Being the king of the fiery suit of Rods, he is passionate and will be sexually active well into later life.

## Reversed Meaning

The old-fashioned attitudes of the upright king take a more bigoted turn when the card is reversed. The fixed opinions of this self-obsessed king may result in him becoming a belligerent bully, possibly with a violent streak. Any advice that this king gives is based on self-interest. This is a man governed by his own desires and passions above anything else.

## Possible Events

If the king of Rods does not symbolize a person, then it speaks of the development of psychological balance and the gaining of wisdom. Ideals and practicalities will merge, enabling you to act with integrity. If reversed, question your motives thoroughly.

# The King of Cups or Hearts

## Description
A mature man, with considerable achievement to his credit. A person of charm and sophistication, fair or gray-haired, with a clear complexion and pale-blue, liquid eyes.

## Upright Meaning
The king of Cups is undoubtedly an attractive man. He is loving and loveable, the life and soul of any gathering. A person of considerable inner strength, he is deeply intuitive. It is likely that in the past he has been through emotionally testing times, but he has come through them a stronger and better person. He is warm-hearted and very loyal. Kindness, generosity, and responsibility are his watchwords. This king enjoys the comforts of life and may be creative. If not, he will certainly appreciate the arts.

RE DI COPPE

## Reversed Meaning
The reversed king of Cups is a rather sad figure, who usually covers up this fact very well. He is likely to be very secretive, yet vulnerable. However, he will tend to take his emotional pain out on others. He may be hot-tempered or possess an "addictive" personality trait – unfortunately, his capacity for self-damage is awesome.

## Possible Events
You may find yourself becoming a mediator between two factions when this card appears. Like a diplomat, you will have to exercise all of your charm to resolve a difficult situation. When this card is reversed, you will find it difficult to persuade rivals to come to an understanding.

RE DI SPADE

# The King of Swords or Spades

## Description

Generally, a tall, dark man with dark-brown eyes. Bear in mind that this card often describes people of varied physical characteristics, so focus instead on the critical role that this person will play in your life.

## Upright Meaning

This is a man of exceptional intelligence and powerful perceptions. The king of Swords symbolizes wisdom and experience, someone in a position of trust and responsibility – a professional advisor, lawyer, or doctor. He will be cool, calm, and collected, disliking any overt displays of emotion, which disturb his mental equilibrium – literally, he lives in his head, happiest in the world of logic and reason. However, due to his brainpower, this king may be easily bored, requiring lots of mental stimulation.

## Reversed Meaning

The reversed king of Swords is a harsh judge and critic of others' actions, yet he tends not to analyze his own. He is a mistrustful person, prone to unfounded suspicions and dark thoughts. He may be a schemer who plays complicated and manipulative mind-games. He could easily be a con man and is certainly deceitful.

## Possible Events

When upright, the king of Swords shows that you will be able to take charge of events and control your life and possibly the lives of others by the force of your will. However, when reversed, the opposite is the case, and you may find yourself feeling controlled and powerless.

RE DI SPADE

# The King of Pentacles or Diamonds

## Description
A dark, often swarthy, mature man, who holds, or has held, a position of considerable responsibility. He may be quite stocky and earthy and may even deal with land or money in some way.

## Upright Meaning
The king of Pentacles is a practical man and in every way a realist. Everything must be grounded in firm fact, so he may choose to work as a bank manager, administrator, or accountant, or, due to the earthy nature of the card, a landowner or farmer. This king is usually married and is financially comfortable. He is shrewd, with a good head for columns of figures. He possesses a stable personality, with a placid temperament, and he is slow to anger.

RE DI DANARI

## Reversed Meaning
When reversed, the king of Pentacles is somewhat foolish and lacking in imagination. He may be corrupt, a person whose word cannot be trusted because he is so easily bribed. This king is a bad enemy to have because he never forgets an offense and always wants to take revenge. He may also associate with gamblers.

## Possible Events
Taking resolute action that will result in financial profit. Self-doubt ends with the appearance of this card, and there will be good fortune in monetary matters and a practical solution to your problems. Dealings with administrators and large institutions are possible. When reversed, strong enemies and rivals are shown, so take care!

## Combinations
Four kings appearing in the same layout can lead to two opposing conclusions, so you'll have to judge for yourself. Either it means that you will be recognized by your peers and gain high achievement when dealing with important matters, or you may become conceited and flushed with your own success. Three kings symbolize the influence of powerful, influential men, while two indicate cooperation and a successful partnership. Note also that one king in a reading has no additional significance, other than the divinatory meaning of the card.

# Cartomancy

# The Art of Reading the Cards

Tarot cards can be read in various ways. Most people use the full deck of 78 cards. Others prefer to use the 22 Major Arcana only. Those who read ordinary playing cards are effectively using the Minor Arcana, so you can use only the Minor Arcana in a Tarot reading, too. Some prefer to do the initial reading with the Major Arcana cards to highlight important issues, following up with spreads utilizing the full pack. Whatever you decide will be the right thing for you to do. Why not experiment? Try out each of the variations in turn to see which one best suits you and your style of card-reading.

# How to Begin

It won't matter whether you are reading the Tarot for yourself or for someone else, because the process for the reader remains the same. A few deep breaths will help to calm the system and clear the mind. Allow yourself to drift into a passive mental state as you shuffle the cards (and if you want to include reversed cards in your reading, remember to turn some as you shuffle. You may also find that you reverse cards instinctively, without making a conscious effort to do so). If you are reading for someone else, the inquirer (old sources call someone who consults the cards "the querent") then shuffles and hands the cards back to you. You can now lay out a number of cards in an appropriate spread. If a specific question is to be asked, then either you or the inquirer should think of this while shuffling. If you find that it helps, you can speak the question out loud before laying out the cards.

# Reading Your Own Cards

Some people think that it is bad luck to read your own cards, but my experience has taught me that it is not so much a matter of luck, but of accuracy, that is at issue. One cannot help but be subjective about one's own life, therefore you will have strong preconceptions about what the cards will say, even before the first one is laid down. You may not understand what the cards are telling you, even if the answer lies before you as plain as the nose on your face. Bearing this in mind, reading for yourself is by no means impossible. However, a good technique is to write down the meanings and positions of the cards for future reference, when they can be interpreted again with a cool head to gain a fuller understanding.

I have found that some spreads are more suitable for reading one's own cards than others. One that is particularly good for this purpose is the four-aces method (see page 110).

# Reading the Cards for Others

Before we move on to individual spreads, you should note that Tarot cards, like most other forms of divinatory tools, tends to focus on drama, or at least on strong emotions, in the life of the person whom you are reading for. This drama may have happened in the past, be occurring now, or will occur in the future. Whenever it is, you can be sure that the cards will home in on it, so don't immediately assume that the appearance of a card such as the ten of Swords or the Tower is a dreadful omen of what is to come. It might just as easily have already happened! So when you start a card reading, it is a good idea not to try to look into the future immediately. Begin by asking the cards about the present. Tell your inquirer what is going on now. If this initial part of the reading is accurate, then it is reasonable to believe that the rest of it will be as well. It is in the art of reading for someone else that the true subtlety of the Tarot cards is revealed. It is only when you can read without preconceptions that you can clearly see what the cards are showing you.

# Past, Present, or Future?

Many Tarot diviners begin a reading by choosing a card to represent the person whom they are reading for. This card is called the "significator," and is usually one of the court cards of the Minor Arcana that most resembles him or her by appearance, role, or career (see pages 84–99). If you can't make up your mind about which king, queen, knight, or page to use, it is traditional to employ as a significator the Magician for a man and the High Priestess for a woman. While this is generally unnecessary if the person is sitting before you, it becomes more important if the person whom you are reading for isn't physically present, because it allows you to focus your intuition on his or her life and fortunes. Some readers even choose a card to represent a question that is asked, such as the ace of Pentacles for a financial query, the Lovers or one of the Cup cards for affairs of the heart. Whether or not you choose to use a significator in this way, its position is indicated on some of the following spreads with an "S."

Reading the cards for someone else brings great responsibility with it. The whole activity is designed to help to clarify issues and to give a guideline for the future. In other words, Tarot cards are meant to help people, not to frighten them! People will take what you say to them very seriously indeed, even if they appear to be skeptical or flippant. It is not your job to upset those who seek your services, so take care when breaking bad news. I tend to think that if one is in doubt about what to say, then say nothing.

# Spreads

Over the centuries, many ways of laying out the cards have been developed. These are called "spreads," and can be of a general nature or extremely specific. If the spread is a general one, then no question is asked and the person reading the cards will gain an overall impression of the events in the inquirer's life and an inkling of the events that will shape the future. General spreads can vary in the number of cards used and in complexity, but these are usually quite large and rather confusing for the beginner. When a direct question is asked, the reader usually employs one of the smaller spreads that tend to be more succinct.

Reading the various patterns that comprise the Tarot spreads is not as difficult as it first appears. The main rule is to take a reading step by step: start at the beginning and continue to the end. If you forget the meaning of a position or a card, then don't be too embarrassed to look it up before you move on to the next one. Remember that the cards will be telling you a story, and that things can become confusing if you start missing out chapters!

Because Tarot beginners are often overwhelmed by having too many cards to read at once, we will begin with some of the simpler layouts before moving on to more complex, general patterns.

*Before attempting a reading, it is vital that the cards are thoroughly mixed together. Even if you aren't good at shuffling, don't rush. Take your time to ensure that the card mix is truly random. If you choose to include reversed cards in your reading, you must turn some around while shuffling.*

# The Three-card Method

This is the most basic form of Tarot divination and can be used as a general reading or in answer to a specific question. Shuffle the cards thoroughly and take the first three cards, face down, from the top of the deck. Lay them out from left to right. This reveals the past, present, and future of a given situation.

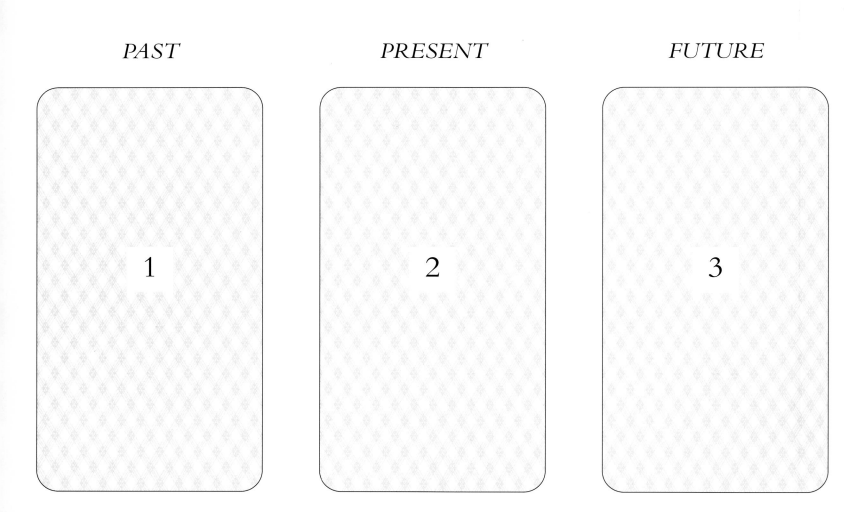

*PAST*  *PRESENT*  *FUTURE*

1    2    3

It is a good idea to become familiar with this basic spread, because variations of it occur in more complex layouts.

# The Simple Cross Spread

This spread is suitable for answering a specific question. It is usual to use the whole Tarot deck of 78 cards. Upright and reversed meanings may be used.

Fist, shuffle the cards while thinking of your question and then lay them out in the shape of a cross, starting at the base. Place an extra card next to the main spread. This extra card (card 6) will represent the overall result.

Card 1. The past and its influence on the present.
Card 2. Obstacles that may be working against your interests.
Card 3. Helpful influences working in your favor.
Card 4. The near future.
Card 5. The more distant future.
Card 6. The eventual outcome and its impact on your life.

After you have finished the reading, if you wish, you can lay out six more cards on top of those in the spread to give added information or to look at events that follow the "outcome" card.

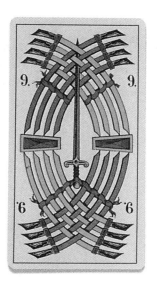

# Three Horseshoe Spreads

This is a very adaptable spread that can be used to answer a specific question. There are many variations of this card pattern, three of which are given here. It is very important to decide which of the variations you want to use before you start – this is dependent on the type of question that is asked. The full Tarot deck or the 22 cards of the Major Arcana may be used, both in upright and reversed positions.

First, choose a significator to represent the person whom you are reading for or the question asked (see pages 84–99). In the diagram, the significator is shown by the card marked with an "S." Shuffle the cards while thinking of your question and then lay them in a pattern in accordance with the diagram.

## The Basic Horseshoe Spread

Card 1. The past and its remaining influence on your question.
Card 2. The present situation.
Card 3. Thing thats you don't know. Hidden influences that have a bearing on your question.
Card 4. Obstacles or difficulties that stand in your way.
Card 5. The attitudes and influences of other people who are relevant to the situation.
Card 6. The best course of action you can take.
Card 7. The eventual outcome in your life.

## The Love Horseshoe Spread

This spread, which is laid out exactly in the same way as the basic horseshoe, is specifically tailored to answer questions of a romantic nature.
Card 1. The foundations of your relationship. The first meeting.
Card 2. The present state of your relationship.
Card 3. Your dreams (or fears) for the future. How you hope your relationship will develop.
Card 4. Conflicts or personality clashes within the relationship.
Card 5. The influence of friends and foes. Is there a rival for your affections?
Card 6. What you should do for the best.
Card 7. The eventual outcome if you take the advice of the previous card.

## The Career Horseshoe Spread

This spread is tailored to career-related dilemmas.
Card 1. The influence of past events on your present question.
Card 2. The present situation as seen from your viewpoint.
Card 3. What is best about the situation.
Card 4. What is worst about the situation.
Card 5. The views of coworkers, bosses, and prevailing financial matters.
Card 6. Your best course of action.
Card 7. The probable result if you take the advice of the previous card.

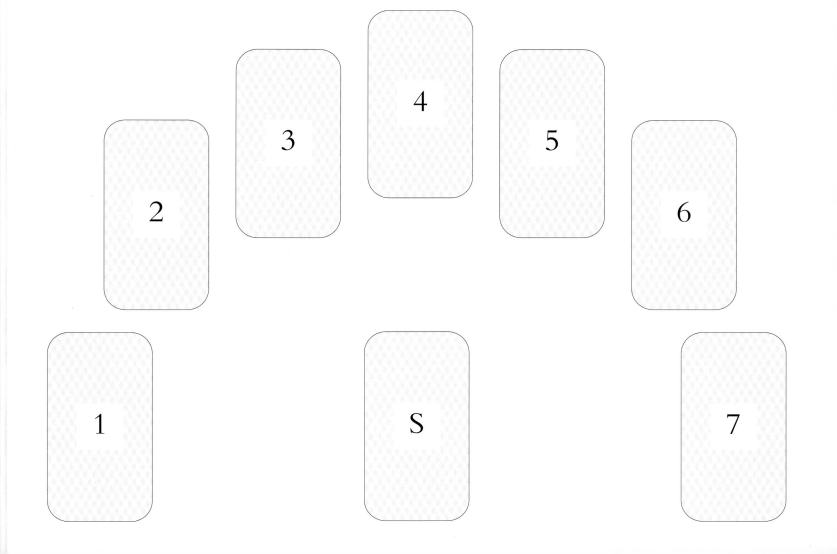

# The Four-aces Method

This more complex spread is particularly suitable for reading one's own cards or as a general reading for someone else. It is an elaboration of the three-card method (page 104). This reading involves the four aces of the Minor Arcana and all of the cards of the Major Arcana. Reversed cards are not generally used in this form of reading.

First, separate the four aces of the Minor Arcana from the rest of the cards. Shuffle them and lay them out in a vertical row, from top to bottom. This process will reveal your order of priorities, from the highest to the lowest. For instance, the ace of Rods will show matters concerning work, career, communications, and anything that requires effort. The ace of Cups reveals your emotional and intimate life, the ace of Swords shows troubles, and the ace of Pentacles uncovers matters of a financial or practical nature (for further information on interpretation, see the four aces, pages 64–65).

Separate the 22 Major Arcana cards from the rest of the deck. Shuffle them thoroughly and choose eight cards. Lay them in turn on either side of each of the aces. In this spread, the aces reveal the topic, while the Major Arcana cards show the past situation on the left and the future on the right, in order of priority.

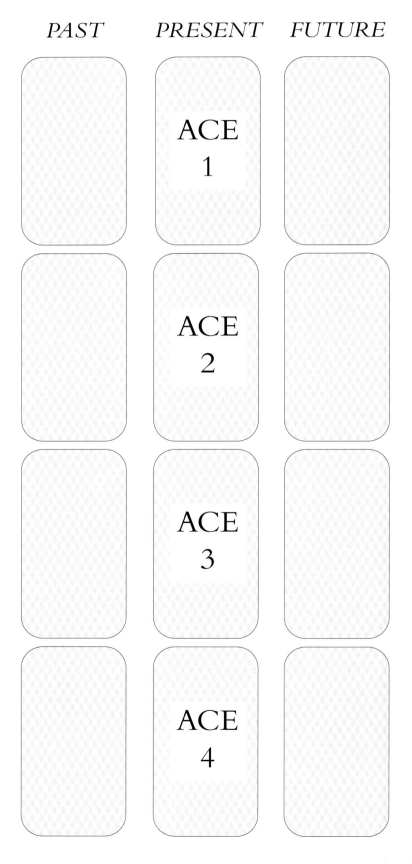

*PAST*  *PRESENT*  *FUTURE*

ACE 1

ACE 2

ACE 3

ACE 4

# The Choices Spread

This layout is very useful if you have to decide between two alternatives, because it points out the possible routes and likely outcomes for each option. We can call them option A and option B. Both the Major and Minor Arcana cards can be used for this spread in upright and reversed positions.

First, choose a significator to represent the questioner or situation, then shuffle the remainder of the pack while thinking about the choice that you have to make. Then lay out the cards in accordance with the diagram.

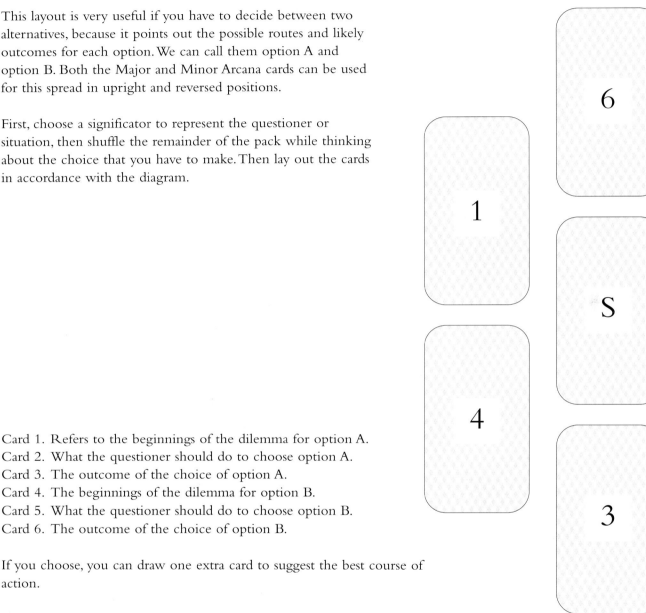

Card 1. Refers to the beginnings of the dilemma for option A.
Card 2. What the questioner should do to choose option A.
Card 3. The outcome of the choice of option A.
Card 4. The beginnings of the dilemma for option B.
Card 5. What the questioner should do to choose option B.
Card 6. The outcome of the choice of option B.

If you choose, you can draw one extra card to suggest the best course of action.

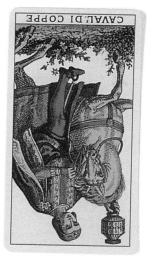

# Timing Spreads

## The Weekly-forecast Spread

This is a useful general spread for forecasting over a short-term period. First, select a significator to occupy the central position, then shuffle the full Tarot deck and deal seven cards in accordance with the diagram. Each card represents one day of the week.

Card 1. Monday.
Card 2. Wednesday.
Card 3. Friday.
Card 4. Sunday.
Card 5. Tuesday.
Card 6. Thursday.
Card 7. Saturday.

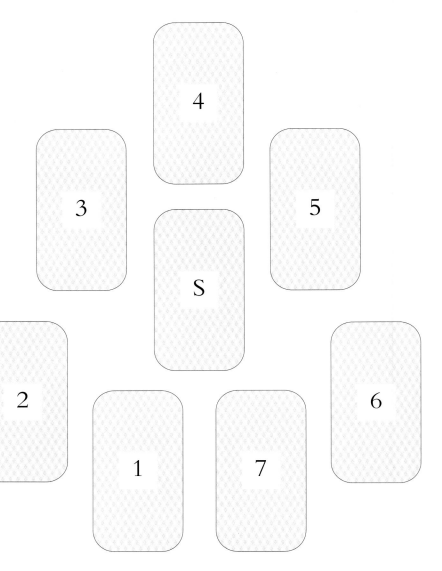

## The Planetary Spread

This is an extension of the weekly-forecast spread, this time using the planets of traditional astrology as the rulers of the days of the week. However, in this case, the cards do not represent time periods, but signify areas of life associated with astrological influences. The process of selecting a significator and dealing the cards is the same as in Figure 6, but with the following interpretation.

Card 1. The position of the Moon. Domestic and family issues.
Card 2. The position of Mercury. Business affairs, skill, and communications.
Card 3. The position of Venus. Love life.
Card 4. The position of the Sun. Achievements, the sense of self.
Card 5. The position of Mars. Opponents, self-assertion, and aggression.
Card 6. The position of Jupiter. Profit, money, gain, and wealth.
Card 7. The position of Saturn. Restrictions, obstacles, and problems.

It is said that if any conflict occurs in the cards, the resolution of this problem will be found in Card 2, the position of Mercury, the mediator.

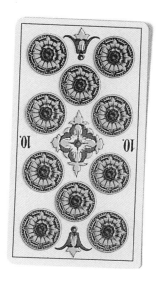

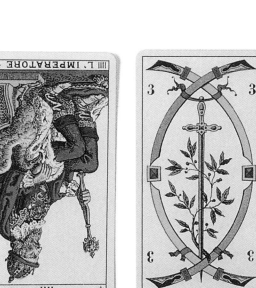

## Timing Spreads

## The Calendar Spread

This general spread gives a forecast for a whole year, month by month. Either the whole Tarot deck is used or just the cards of the Minor Arcana. If only the Minor Arcana cards are employed, then it is traditional to place two cards in each position to represent one month starting. In both cases, begin at Card 1, which represents the month of the time of the reading. The thirteenth or central card will provide a general overview of your fortunes for the year ahead.

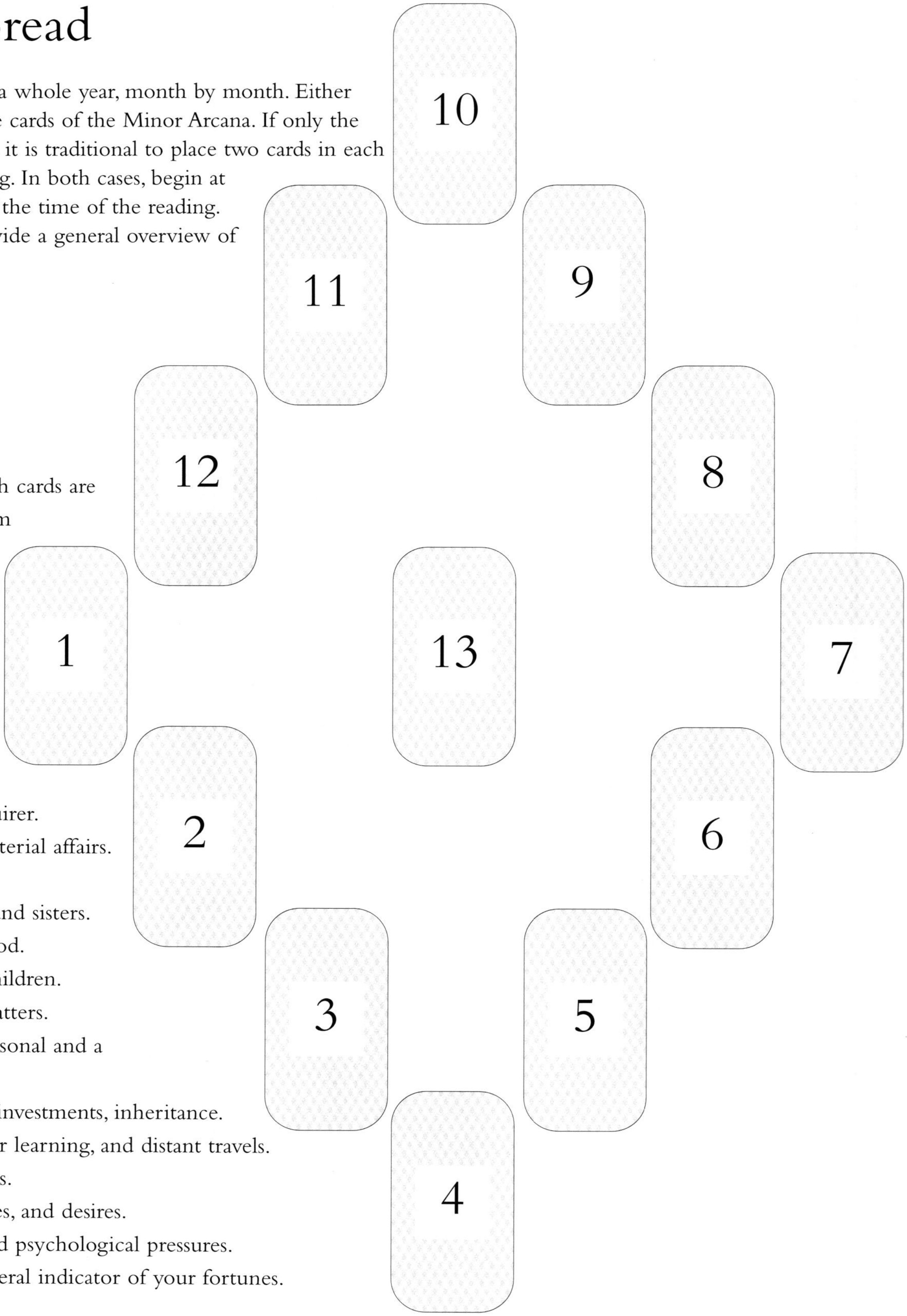

## The Horoscope Spread

This is another general spread, in which cards are laid out in accordance with the diagram shown. In this case, the houses of the astrological horoscope provide the inspiration. Each card position occupies a "House," symbolizing a sphere of life. As with the calendar spread, two cards may be used in each position for added information.

Card 1.  The personality of the inquirer.
Card 2.  Money, possessions, and material affairs.
Card 3.  Learning, short journeys, communications, brothers and sisters.
Card 4.  Home life, origins, childhood.
Card 5.  Romance, creativity, fun, children.
Card 6.  Work, habits, and health matters.
Card 7.  Relationships of both a personal and a business nature.
Card 8.  Sexuality, shared resources, investments, inheritance.
Card 9.  Religion, philosophy, higher learning, and distant travels.
Card 10.  Career, status, and ambitions.
Card 11.  Friendships, social life, hopes, and desires.
Card 12.  Secrets, hidden enemies, and psychological pressures.
Card 13.  (The central card). The general indicator of your fortunes.

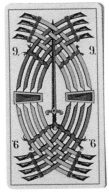

# The Big-wheel Spread

In this, the last Tarot spread of the book, we return to an elaboration of the most basic Tarot layout – the three-card spread. Essentially, this card pattern is ten three-card spreads, each referring to a different area of life to be read in the past, present, future sequence. These will be generally called Group 1, Group 2 etc. Though the big wheel is usually used as a general-type spread, it can also be used thoroughly to answer a given question in detail.

Step 1. Choose a significator to occupy the central position, then shuffle and deal the cards in groups of three, in accordance with the diagram.

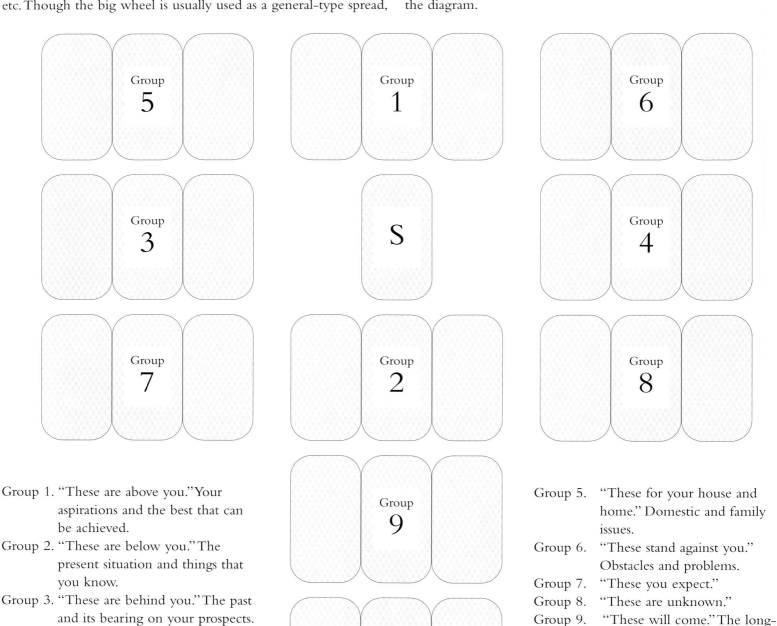

Group 1. "These are above you." Your aspirations and the best that can be achieved.

Group 2. "These are below you." The present situation and things that you know.

Group 3. "These are behind you." The past and its bearing on your prospects.

Group 4. "These are before you." The short-term future prospects.

Group 5. "These for your house and home." Domestic and family issues.

Group 6. "These stand against you." Obstacles and problems.

Group 7. "These you expect."

Group 8. "These are unknown."

Group 9. "These will come." The long-term prospects.

Group 10. "These are sure to be." The outcome and distant future.

# Timing Your Reading

# How to Time Your Reading

Most aspiring Tarot readers soon get to grips with the various layouts for the cards, and will quite quickly be able to deliver accurate interpretations. However, you can progress from foretelling events to saying when these events are likely to occur. There are a number of techniques to help you to do this. You can use layouts specifically designed to predict events within a certain time frame, such as the calendar spread or weekly spread (see pages 114–17).

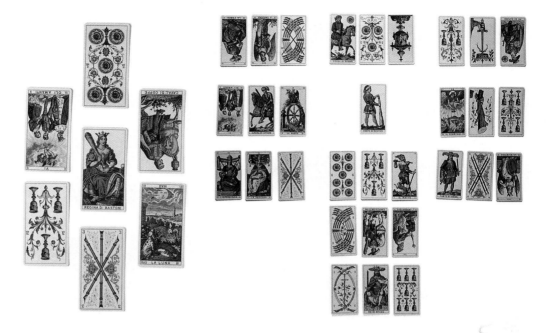

However, you can use the methods below to time any other spread that you have already laid out, such as the simple cross spread (see page 106) or the horseshoe spread (see page 108).

# Timing With the Major Arcana

If you have created a reading using only the Major Arcana, then the astrological attributions may be helpful. Turning an extra card could reveal a whole set of associations, one of which will probably be a sign of the zodiac. For example, if you wish to know when an event will occur and you turn up the Emperor, then there is a connection with the sign of Aries, the Ram (March 21 to April 20). If the Devil turns up, then it can be related to the sign of Capricorn (December 22 to January 20). Because star signs begin and end on specific dates, this will give you a good indication of the timing of the reading. Of course, not all Major Arcana cards are associated with the signs of the zodiac, so this method cannot be used in all cases. Here is a list of Major Arcana cards that can be used as timing indicators, with the dates of their associated zodiac signs.

*If the Major Arcana is used as a tool for timing a reading, the astrological attributions of the cards provide useful guides. The Emperor relates to the sign of Aries and would indicate an event happening between March 21 and April 20. The Devil, on the other hand, being related to the sign of Capricorn, would indicate an event occurring between December 22 and January 20.*

| No. | Card Title | Astrological Sign | Dates |
|---|---|---|---|
| IV | The Emperor | Aries, the Ram | March 21–April 20 |
| V | The Hierophant | Taurus, the Bull | April 21–May 20 |
| VI | The Lovers | Gemini, the Twins | May 22–June 21 |
| VII | The Chariot | Cancer, the Crab | June 22–July 23 |
| XI | Strength★ | Leo, the Lion | July 24–Aug. 23 |
| IX | The Hermit | Virgo, the Virgin | Aug. 24–Sept. 23 |
| VIII | Justice★ | Libra, the Scales | Sept 24–Oct. 23 |
| XIII | Death | Scorpio, the Scorpion | Oct. 24–Nov. 22 |
| XIV | Temperance | Sagittarius, the Archer | Nov. 23–Dec. 21 |
| XV | The Devil | Capricorn, the Goat | Dec. 22–Jan. 20 |
| XVII | The Star | Aquarius, the Waterbearer | Jan 21–Feb. 19 |
| XVIII | The Moon | Pisces, the Fish | Feb. 20–March 20 |

★ See page 13 (Major Arcana introduction).

In addition to this, Major Arcana cards can indicate seasonal time periods. The Empress may indicate the season of spring, the Sun may suggest summer, and the Moon may show a lunar cycle of 28 days. Quite apart from their astrological significance, the Hermit may hint at winter because of its association with old age, and the Star may point to Christmas.

# Timing With the Minor Arcana

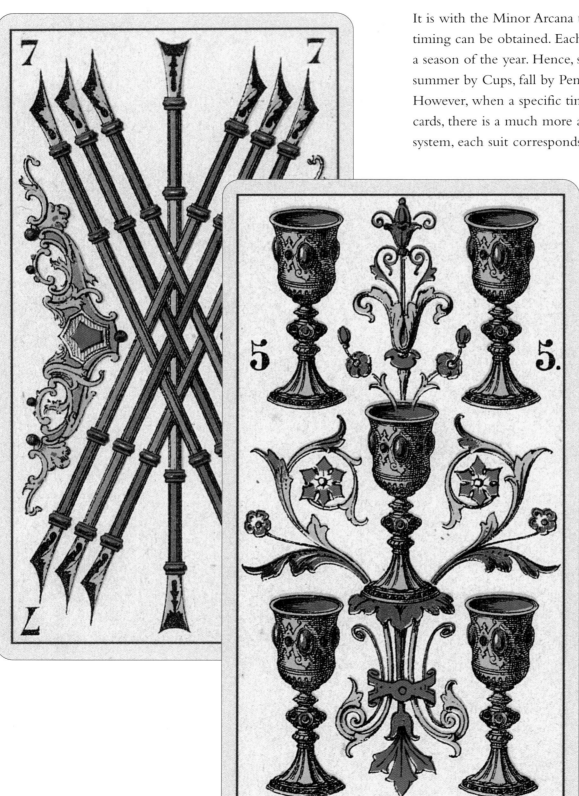

It is with the Minor Arcana that the greatest accuracy in Tarot timing can be obtained. Each of the four suits is associated with a season of the year. Hence, spring is represented by Rods, summer by Cups, fall by Pentacles, and winter by Swords. However, when a specific timing question has been asked of the cards, there is a much more accurate method available. In this system, each suit corresponds to a different measurement of time. Pentacles represent years, Swords indicate months, Rods are weeks, and Cups are days (but only if the Cup card is next to a Pentacle, otherwise it is ignored). To use this technique, count backward from the last card that you laid down, disregarding all Major Arcana and court cards, and note the first numbered Minor Arcana card that you come to. This card gives the time period that you are looking for. For example, if the last card laid down is the six of Swords, then the time period would be six months; if it were the six of Rods, then it would be six weeks. The ace of Swords would signify one month, whereas the eight of Pentacles would indicate a time period of eight years, and so on.

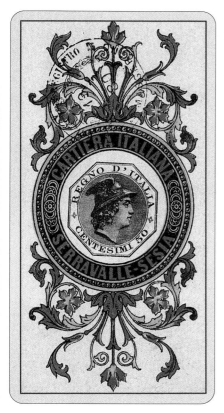

Pentacles = Years

Swords = Months

Wands = Weeks

The Tarot speaks to us on many levels at once, and beginners may become confused by the wealth of information that a single card can deliver. The four aces, for instance, not only represent the ancient elements of Earth, Air, Fire, and Water, but can also symbolize the seasons and provide a valuable tool for timing a predictive forecast. Of course, this holds true for the other numbered cards in the Minor Arcana as well. However, when dealing with the Pentacle cards, some leeway must be given: after all, the ten of that suit would technically foretell a period of ten years, when, in actuality, it is merely indicating a long time without being too literal about the actual number of years. The Cups may not indicate any time period at all, unless, of course, they are next to a Pentacle card, in which case they show a number of days. Rods and Swords are usually the most accurate indicators of the passage of time and are rarely inaccurate.

Cups = Days (these do not count unless the Cup card is directly next to a Pentacle).

# Index

IL BAGATTO

This book is dedicated to Muriel

## Acknowledgements

With sincere gratitude to Sasha Fenton, Jan Budkowski, Liz Dean, and Bruce Cooke. Their words of wisdom and technical expertise have been invaluable. Also thanks to Grant Griffiths, Mari Griffith, and Jonah for being good friends.

## Bibliography

*Cartomancy,* Alessandro Bellenghi. English edition (Ebury Press, 1988).
*The Devil's Picture Book,* Paul Hudson. (Sphere Books, 1972).
*Fortune Telling by Tarot Cards,* Sasha Fenton. (Thorsons, 1985).
*Tarot in Action,* Sasha Fenton. (The Aquarian Press, 1987).
*Super Tarot,* Sasha Fenton. (The Aquarian Press, 1991).
*The Book of Thoth,* Aleister Crowley. (Samuel Weiser Inc., 1969).
*Tarotmania,* Jan Woudhuysen. (Sphere Books, 1981).
*Tarot,* Jane Lyle. (Hamlyn, 1990).
*The Tarot,* Richard Cavendish. (Michael Joseph, 1975).
*Tarot,* Jonathan Dee. (Paragon, 1996).

The cards on page 8 are from the Dee-Loren deck, Jonathan Dee.
All other Tarot decks and cards: Lo Scarabeo, Torino, Italy.